19th Century American Clocks

Books by H. G. Harris

Handbook of Watch and Clock Repairs
Advanced Watch and Clock Repair
Collecting and Identifying Old Clocks
Collecting and Identifying Old Watches

19TH CENTURY AMERICAN CLOCKS

H. G. HARRIS

1981

EMERSON BOOKS, INC.
Buchanan, New York 10511

Published by Emerson Books, Inc.
Library of Congress Catalog Card Number 81 - 65124
International Standard Book Number 87523 - 197 - 7

CONTENTS

ACKNOWLEDGMENTS

The author wishes to thank those who kindly gave permission for their photographs to be reproduced in this book, and to thank Antoinette Campbell-Hunter for producing the artwork and line drawings.

Figures: 4,5,8,10-12,14, 16-18,21,22,25-28,35, 53-56,59,60	by courtesy of the Henry Francis du Pont Winterthur Museum, Winterthur, Delaware.
Figures: 6,20	by courtesy of Museum of Art, Carnegie Institute, Pittsburgh, Pennsylvania.
Figures: 7,19,23,24,38,58	by courtesy of The Baltimore Museum of Art, Baltimore, Maryland.
Figures: 9,13	by courtesy of The Daughters of the American Revolution Museum. Photography by Helga Photo Studio.
Figures: 31,32,32A,33, 33A,36,37,42-45,46, 46A,51,61	by courtesy of Illinois State Museum, Springfield, Illinois.
Figures: 39,48-50,62	by courtesy of Antique Imports, Frederick, Maryland. Photography by Bruce C. DeGrange.
Figures: 47,52,57	by courtesy of Sotheby Park Bernet, Inc., Madison Avenue, New York.

INTRODUCTION

AFTER THE publication of *Collecting and Identifying Old Clocks* many readers suggested that there should be a companion book dealing only with American clocks, and so this book was written.

The period 1800 to 1900 is a convenient one. Prior to 1800 the only clocks made in America in any quantity were grandfather clocks and Massachusetts shelf clocks. After 1900 the traditional American style of clock gave way to more modern and universal designs where price was of paramount importance.

During the first fifty years of the nineteenth century the American clock industry made great and rapid strides, both in design and in method of production, so much so that the rest of the world acclaimed the Connecticut clockmakers as leaders in the field of mass production methods. This is reflected by the many countries who copied American techniques.

When studying these old clocks, not only are we bound to learn about the mechanisms and the cases in which they are housed, but for many readers there will be as much, if not more, interest shown in the men who made them and the extraordinary genius that led to their revolutionary methods.

Frequently one will find a clock by an unknown maker whose place of origin, displayed on the dial or clockpaper, is one's own home town. That in itself can be the beginning of a search into local history. An article in the town newspaper asking for information from anyone who knows the whereabouts of descendants of the maker can sometimes provide sufficient information to start a succession of inquiries. There are other sources of local information such as public libraries, registrars of births and deaths, churches and newspaper offices.

Occasionally one meets members of the family who, through the years, have inherited one or more clocks by this maker. The original workshop premises might still be standing, although used for a different purpose. The local newspaper might well be interested in the search, particularly so if the makings of a story begin to emerge.

In itself, the search can be a pleasant and interesting pastime that can lead to who knows where.

On the other hand, anyone who has a few tools and can find a clock in need of some repair, will have the enjoyment of restoring it to a condition more closely resembling the original. The result can only be pride of ownership and investment. In this respect, Chapters 6 and 7 should prove helpful as will the list of suppliers at the end of Chapter 6.

I hope you will find as much enjoyment in your searching as I have had over the years.

H.G. HARRIS

PREFACE

DURING the early years of the seventeenth century the first domestic clocks were brought into the American colonies by wealthy families and government officials from England. These clocks were the lantern type.

The majority of towns had provided themselves with a public bell, installed in a church tower or government building, which was tolled at each hour of the day for the benefit of the community.

The earliest recorded weight-driven striking clocks were installed in English Abbeys, cathedrals and churches from about 1280. Among the earliest known large public clocks are those of St Paul's Cathedral, London, 1286; Canterbury Cathedral, England, 1292; Exeter Cathedral, England, 1300; Milan Cathedral, Italy, 1335; Salisbury Cathedral, England, 1386; Rouen Cathedral, France, 1389; Wells Cathedral, England, 1392. Of these, only Salisbury, Rouen and Wells have been preserved. The Salisbury clock can be seen in the nave of the Cathedral, and the Wells clock is on view in the Science Museum, London.

These early clocks were made of iron and each piece was heated in an open forge and hand-beaten to shape on an anvil by a blacksmith. Parts that required more accurate shaping were finished by filing. When the clocks were assembled they took the form of an open box frame measuring a few feet wide. The assembley was usually held together by iron wedges or pins.

The rate at which these clocks were allowed to run down was controlled by a verge and crown wheel escapement, and the strike mechanism was controlled by the locking plate system. The principles of operation of these two mechanisms have remained unchanged.

It was not until about 1665 that the first tower clocks were imported from England and Europe.

In the meantime, at The Hague in 1657, the Dutch scientist Christiaan Huygens applied the principle of a pendulum to a clock movement with remarkable results. Never before had a timepiece been made that was capable of such near accuracy. Following this discovery mantel clocks appeared in England in 1658 and tall case clocks in 1659, but it was not until about 1685 that tall case clocks were first brought to the American colonies.

It is known that there were clock and watch repairers from England and Europe at work in the colonies by about 1690, but it was not until the early years of the eighteenth century that clockmakers and watchmakers came to America. There is evidence to suggest some of the repairers imported clocks and watches from England and Europe and sold them under their own names. It is almost certain that watches were not made in America until about 1850 but it is possible that imported parts may have been assembled.

The first tall case clock made in the colonies seems to be about 1695. Those that followed were typically English in style but lacking the quality of workmanship for which the English makers had become renowned.

The early eighteenth century clockmakers worked under difficult conditions. Everything they needed they had to make themselves while possessing only a very limited range of simple tools and a blacksmith's forge. Metal was scarce and every piece of unwanted brass was melted down. Molds were made with sand, and rough movement plates and blanks for wheels were cast. When the metal was cool it had to be hardened by a long process of light hammering known as planishing. The metal was then filed flat to the required thickness and turned to the required diameter. The wheel blanks were marked to show the positions of teeth and each tooth was laboriously filed. The successful men were those who had served an apprenticeship and who had become craftsmen in their own right.

To make an eight-day brass movement under these conditions took many months of hard patient work and to its cost had to be added that of the case.

These early clocks were usually made to order for wealthy families, and where there was wealth the clockmakers settled.

Later in the eighteenth century, dials, tools, materials and movement parts were imported from England and Europe, but even so the amount of hand work required to complete a movement was still considerable.

Then came the War of American Independence that lasted from 1775 until 1783. During those eight years the manufacture of clocks was almost at a standstill while the makers directed their efforts to the requirements of war.

The revolution resulted in supplies from England being stopped. Brass in America was scarce and expensive and so a cheaper and more readily available material had to be found. Clockmakers turned to wood, and new styles and techniques began to emerge.

The first serious attempt was made about 1798 by Gideon Roberts who, assisted by his sons, set up a factory at Bristol near Plymouth, Connecticut, and produced thirty-hour wood movements in small batches. Wood movements had been made before, particularly by Benjamin Cheyney, Jr., from about 1745, but they were large and a little primitive and were individually made.

Makers of brass movements were able to cut small teeth in the rims of wheel blanks which kept the wheel diameters to a minimum. Wheels and pinions were mounted on arbors made from thin steel rod and the components were assembled and held in place between brass plates of minimum thickness.

Such was not the case when working with wood. Selected hardwoods were used, but even so the fibrous nature of wood demanded larger and thicker teeth which meant an increase in the size of the wheel blanks. Similarly, the wood arbors had to be increased in diameter and the plates made thicker.

Changes in temperature and humidity frequently caused distortion in the components which in turn affected the performance of the movement. This problem had to be taken into account when choosing the wood and when determining the size and shape of each piece that was to be made.

The result of all this was a movement larger than its brass counterpart, and when tall case clock cases were made for these movements it was sometimes necessary to design the hoods a little larger than would have been required for a brass movement.

During the first ten years of the nineteenth century, clockmakers continued making cases and movements by hand. Then, in 1810, Eli Terry showed Americans how to mass produce thirty-hour wood movements with interchangeable parts by the thousands in a fraction of the time taken by hand and at a cost considerably less than anyone else had ever achieved.

Movements were of little use without cases and by 1819 Terry had introduced the pillar and scroll clock and had set up a production line in his factory turning out cases in large quantities.

Terry's achievments revolutionized the industry. Hand crafting was out. There was a rush for property where water power could be harnessed. Factories sprang into being and despite Terry's patents, other makers copied his design while others, a little more cautious, avoided infringement of patent rights by making small changes in design.

Many business transactions took place without the need for money. Makers exchanged movements for cases, and cases for movements, thereby enabling them to assemble complete clocks which were sold under their own names. Capital for machinery was raised by mortgaging property or by entering into a partnership. The industry began to boom, and for the first time clocks became available to a wide section of the population.

In 1830 the industry was given another tremendous impetus by Joseph Ives who introduced an eight-day brass movement capable of being manufactured by mass production methods.

Before the industry had adjusted itself to the idea that the era for wood movements was over, Joseph Shaylor Ives, in 1836, invented a method of making coil springs of brass. Makers were now able to produce wood cases and spring driven brass movements by mass production methods. An entirely new approach to clockmaking had been opened up.

The following year, in 1837, a financial crisis swept across the country. The value of the dollar fell dramatically and many banks were forced to close. Businesses all over the country suffered and clockmakers were no exception. Many went bankrupt.

In 1838 Chauncey Jerome introduced a cheap one-day brass movement in an Ogee case that sold for about one dollar and fifty cents. It was an immediate success and very large quantities were sold. In 1842 Jerome shipped the first of many consignments to England, and it was from this small beginning that clocks became one of America's biggest exports.

By 1845 Connecticut clockmakers achieved world supremacy in clock production. The output was approximately one million a year, most of which came from Bristol and surrounding towns. Coiled springs were taking over from weights giving case makers new freedom of design. Then, about 1849, the spring balance wheel or marine movement was introduced offering advantages over a pendulum controlled movement. In 1875 the spring balance wheel movement was fitted to small alarm clocks in round cases, and tens of thousands were shipped all over the world.

The story of nineteenth century American clocks begins with the continued popularity of grandfather clocks, even though they had been in use one hundred and twenty years, and continues with the introduction of hand made wall and shelf clocks followed by factory, mass produced clocks.

CHAPTER 1

Acquiring an Old Clock

FOR MOST OF US, the only way to acquire an old clock is to buy one, but there is always that element of doubt before parting with our money. Is the clock worth the price being asked? There is only one satisfactory way of finding out and that is to submit the clock to a close inspection, noting as much information as possible, and then seeking the advice of a reputable dealer, or an experienced collector.

If the person selling is a dealer with a good reputation, then you may be prepared to accept his assessment of the value. If the clock is being offered for sale by auction, then a professional valuation is advisable before bidding takes place.

Factors that influence the value of an old clock are: type of clock — they may be scarce or plentiful; maker — famous or well known will realize a higher price; age of clock; general condition; previous owners, if well known; whether or not it will run; amount of restoration work required.

Regardless of whether the clock is being sold privately, or by auction or being offered for sale in a shop, the seller can hardly refuse a potential purchaser permission to examine the clock on the premises, unless of course there is something to hide, in which case it would probably be better not to pursue the matter.

When a dealer is interested in a clock being offered for sale he can fall back on his experience. He will spend a few minutes closely examining the clock for genuine antiquity and condition and will be able to form an opinion of its market value immediately. Whether or not a sale takes place will depend on that knowledge.

A beginner cannot hope to deal with such a situation in the same way, and it would be most unwise for him to try. He should tell the seller that he wishes to examine the clock, make notes, and go away to think the matter over.

If your knowledge of old America clocks enables you to identify the type of clock being sold, it is an advantage. If not, a few notes describing its shape, design and size will be necessary for later identification. A Polaroid photograph would be even better.

If the clock is weight driven, or pendulum controlled, or is hanging on a wall, or is otherwise too big or heavy to handle, then the inspection must be carried out without interference to the clock. A small pocket flashlight is very useful when inspecting inside the case. If the clock is not runnning ask to see it put in motion.

Fakes are sometimes offered for sale as the genuine article, and they are not always easy to detect. One simple test of age, which on its own is far from conclusive, is to smell the movement. Old and rancid clock oil, shut up in a case for many years, has a most distinctive and rather unpleasant smell. This is something that cannot be faked.

It is suggested the inspection be carried out in the following order: case exterior, case interior, dial and hands, and movement.

The items listed below are those that would help in establishing the identity of the clock and assessing its value.

Case exterior

1. General condition
2. Type of finish
   - Paint
   - Stain
   - Polish
3. Decoration
   - Carving
   - Stencilling
   - Special molding
   - Mirror
   - Reverse painted glass tablet
   - Veneer

Case interior

4. General condition
5. Layout
   Method of supporting movement
   Position of line pulleys
   Any wood partitions
6. Details of clock paper
   Maker's name and location
   Any setting up instructions
7. Details of any repairs or cleaning. These are sometimes written on the back of the outside of the case.
   Dates
   Repairer's name
8. Any indication of previous ownership such as an engraved presentation plate.

Dial and hands

9. Write down any wording there may be on the dial
10. Endeavor to identify the type of dial
    Printed paper glued to metal
    Printed paper glued to wood
    Painted metal
    Painted wood
    Enamel on metal
11. Try to identify the hands as being:
    Stamped from thin sheet metal, or
    Hand cut from thick material
12. Note any additional dial information, such as:
    Center sweep hand
    Small seconds hand
    Details of any calendar information and method of presentation.
13. Method used to fix dial to movement

Movement

14. General condition

15. Wood or brass
16. Type of plates
    - Full
    - Strap
    - Pierced
    - Ladder
17. Motive power
    - Weight
    - Wagon spring
    - Coiled spring
18. Control
    - Pendulum
    - Spring balance
19. With or without fusee
20. Type of pinions
    - Roller
    - Lantern
    - Leaves
21. Type of strike
    - Rack and snail
    - Locking plate or count wheel
22. Pendulum
    - Centrally positioned
    - Off center
    - Length
23. Run of weight lines

The list may look formidable and circumstances could well make it impossible to complete, but it does indicate the extent to which an inspection is often necessary to establish identity.

Once away from the premises in which the clock is housed, the notes can be studied closely. Providing the name of the maker is known, reference can be made to the list of makers contained in the books shown in Appendix 4, which are usually available in public libraries. These lists show against each name the dates when the clockmaker was in business or his life span. That will be the first step towards finding the approximate age of the clock.

The remaining details noted at the inspection can be compared with the information given in the following chapters, and a closer assessment of age may well be obtained.

A detailed knowledge of the history of the particular type of clock will often indicate whether it was produced in large quantities or whether it is likely to be scarce, in which case it might have a more favorable value as a collectors' piece.

When your research is complete and your notes rewritten, take them to a dealer and ask for his opinion. If he wants to charge a nominal fee for his services, this is not unreasonable. It may prevent you from paying too high a price for the clock.

CHAPTER 2

Tall Case Clocks

AMERICAN TALL CASE clocks, or grandfather clocks as they are popularly known, were first made about 1695 in Pennsylvania and Massachusetts, and a little later in Connecticut, after which the craft spread to surrounding states. Throughout their life span there were probably more tall case clocks made in Pennsylvania than in any other state.

From 1690 until The War of Independence in 1775, they closely resembled the English style. When the war ended in 1783 casemakers began introducing their own styles which, by the end of the eighteenth century, were well established.

Nineteenth century tall case clocks are not necessarily better than their predecessors. In fact, there are many examples of eighteenth century clocks being superior in craftsmanship and design, particularly among those made to special order.

At the beginning of the nineteenth century, makers took a more active interest in small and less expensive clocks produced by factory methods, and about 1805 there began a decline in the number of tall case clocks made until about 1840, after one hundred and fifty years, the making of tall case clocks came to an end. Nevertheless, these nineteenth century clocks are very much collectors' pieces and are no less sought after than are their predecessors.

Cases and Dials

During the nineteenth century there were no important changes in the design of cases. Mahogany continued to be the most used wood, either in solid form or as a veneer, and pine, walnut and birch were also widely used.

The more expensive cases were frequently decorated with inlay work of satinwood, cherry and maple, whereas the cheaper cases were given little or no decoration and were often made of pine or painted pine. Cases decorated with marquetry or Japanning are rare.

The height of cases to the top of the center finial can be anything from about six feet, nine inches to nine feet.

It was about 1800 when clock papers were first printed. The casemaker and movement maker each glued their label inside the case.The labels were printed with the name and town of the maker. Frequently the address and year of manufacture were also given. The clockmaker's label also provided winding and setting up instructions, maintenance instructions, and sometimes announced details of after-sales service. These labels or clock papers provide a starting point for obtaining identification and age of the clock.

The majority of clocks were fitted with a break-arch dial, and the lower edge of the hood pediment was correspondingly shaped. The shape of the top of the hood pediment is usually break-arch or scrolls, both of which are frequently decorated with frets and finials, the finials being turned or carved wood, or brass. At each front corner of the hood is a wood column which can be plain, baluster, Jacobean or Corinthian. The Corinthian columns were sometimes fitted with brass capitals. Identical columns were frequently fitted at the rear corners of the hood and matching quarter columns on the front corners of the trunk and the plinth.

To gain access to the movement the hood has to be removed by sliding it forward off the trunk. A door is provided in the trunk through which the pendulum, weights and lines can be reached. Clocks fitted with wood pull-up movements are wound through the door aperture.

Before 1780 nearly all tall case clocks were fitted with break-arch dials, the majority of which were made of brass and elaborately engraved. These dials were expensive to make, and about 1780 makers started importing hand painted metal and wood dials from England at much reduced prices. The numerals

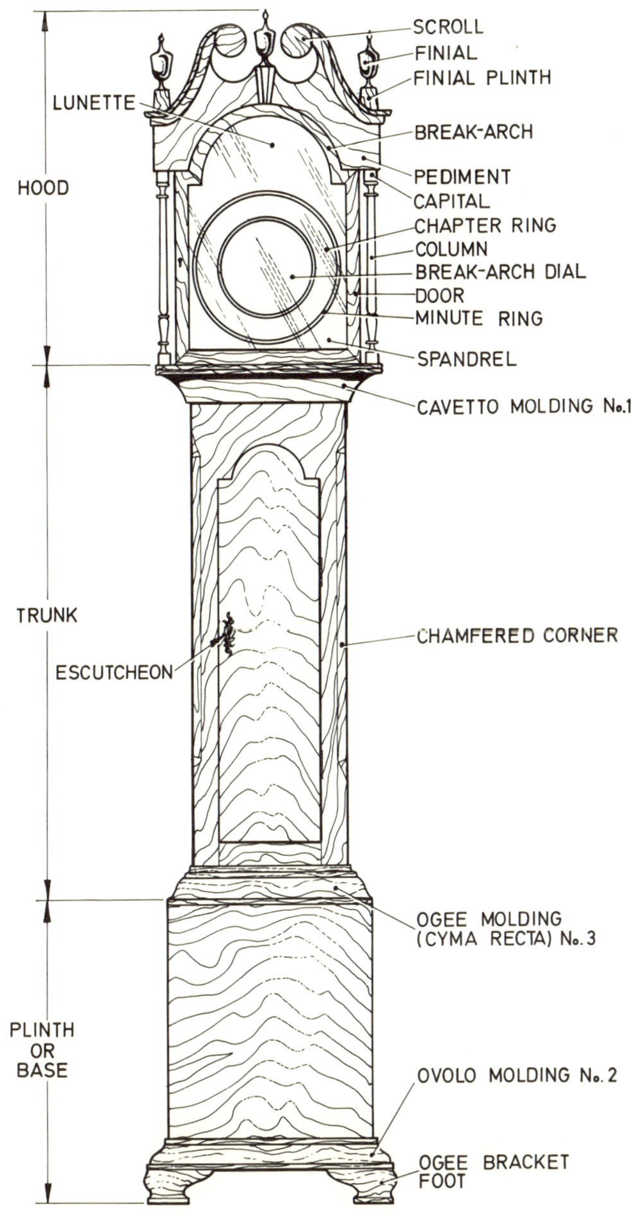

Figure 1. Tall case.

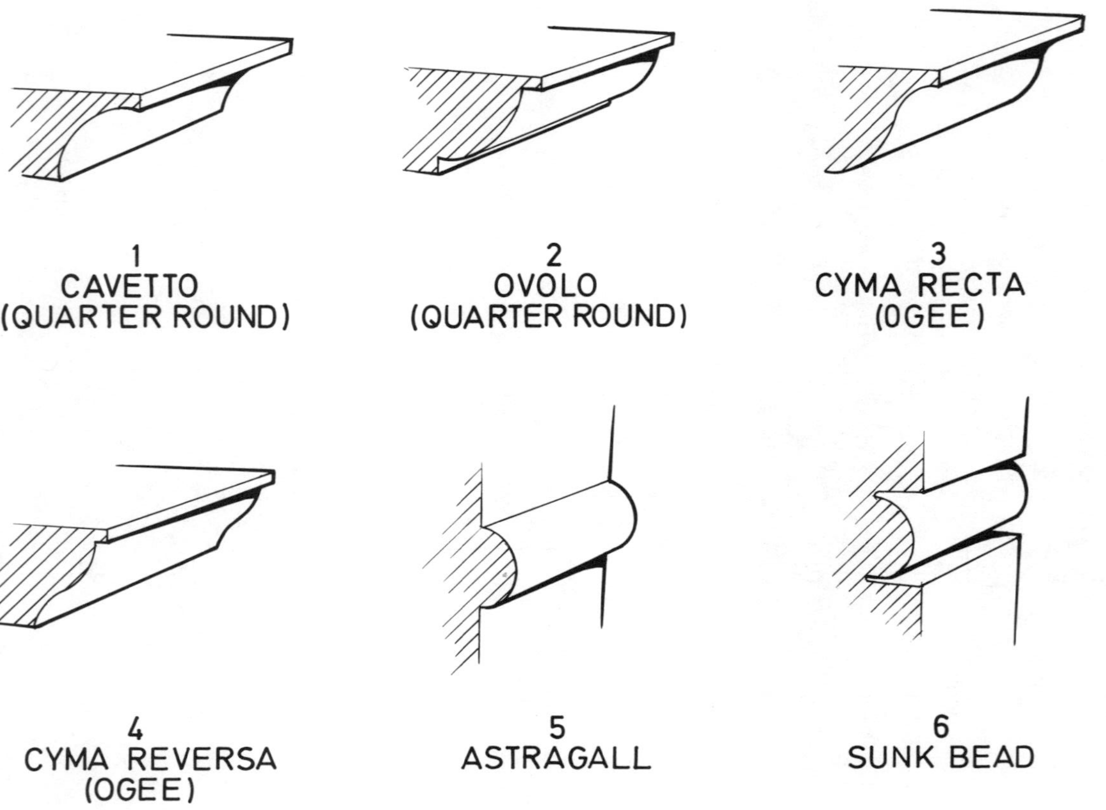
1
CAVETTO
(QUARTER ROUND)
2
OVOLO
(QUARTER ROUND)
3
CYMA RECTA
(OGEE)
4
CYMA REVERSA
(OGEE)
5
ASTRAGALL
6
SUNK BEAD

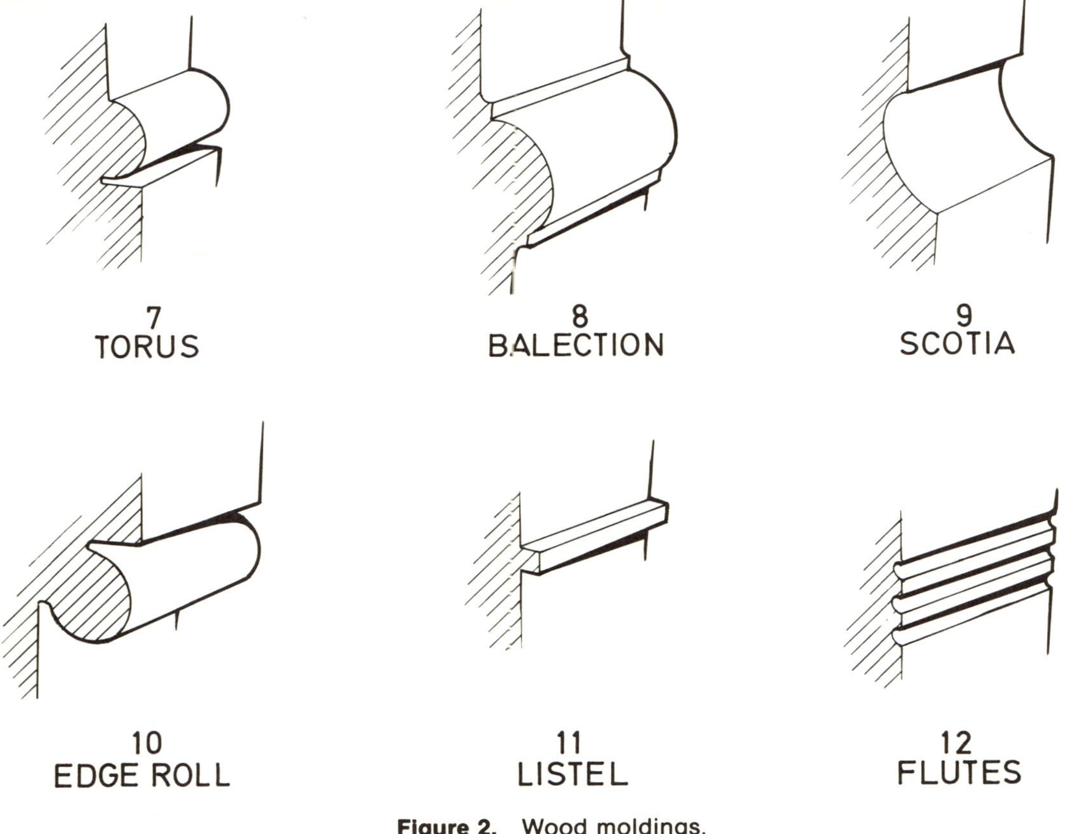

Figure 2. Wood moldings.

and divisions are black against a background of white. The spandrels are decorated with figures, flowers, birds, fruit, scrolls and geometric or foliage designs, while the lunette can contain pastoral scenes, landscapes, seascapes, buildings and animals in a variety of colors. A further embellishment, with a strong novelty appeal, is the use of automata in the lunette. Typical examples are a lady on a swing, a fisherman casting his line, a rocking ship and a blacksmith at his anvil, all of which are caused to move by the action of the pendulum. With the importation of dials came the introduction of Arabic numerals in the chapter ring which previously had contained only Roman numerals.

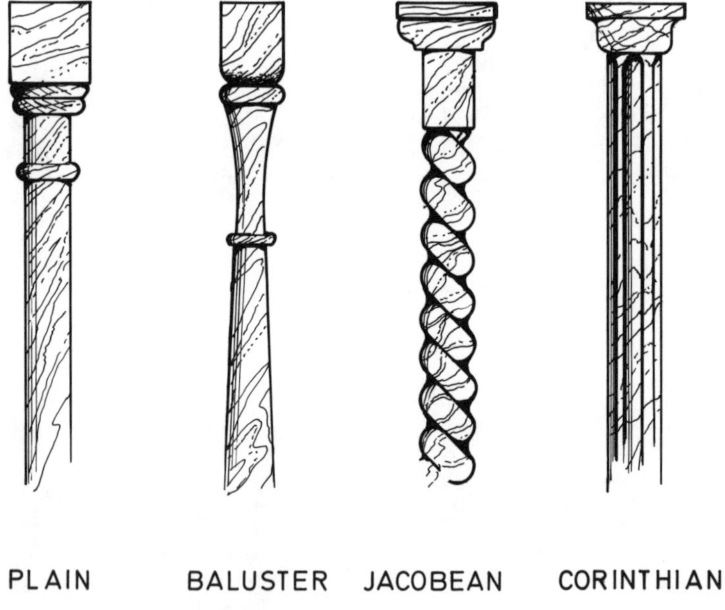

Figure 3. Wood columns.

Figure 4.

Figure 4. 8-day, mahogany, striking, tall case clock. Circa 1790 - 1815. Simon Willard, Roxbury, Mass. Pine case veneered with mahogany and inlaid with satinwood. The hood pediment is a true break-arch. Mounted on the top is a fret and 3 turned brass finials on square plinths. At each front corner of the hood stands a plain turned and kerfed wood column with brass capitals. At the top and bottom of the trunk is a cavetto molding and at each front corner is a quarter column to match those on the hood. A Simon Willard printed label is adhered to the inside of the trunk door. The plinth has a straight molded skirt and ogee bracket feet. Height 88 inches. The dial was made and painted by James Wilson, Birmingham, England. The name Wilson is cast into the false iron plate behind the dial. In the break-arch is a painting of a girl sitting beside a birdcage while painted flowers decorate the spandrels. The dial has a small seconds subsidiary dial and a curved date aperture. The hour and minute hands are pierced and filed. Painted on the dial is the signature Simon Willard. The movement is 8-day with anchor escapement and rack and snail strike system.

(Right)

Figure 5. 8-day, walnut, striking tall case clock. Circa 1790 - 1825. David Oyster, Reading, Pa. This is a particularly fine case, tastefully decorated, and has the appearance of being made for an important person. The case is entirely of walnut and without inlay work, the decoration being confined to wood beading, low relief carving and medallions. The top of the pediment carries two carved scrolls terminating in rosettes and three turned wood finials each supported by its own plinth. Beneath the center finial is an eagle. The inner edge of the break-arch door is beaded and the four corners of the hood carry fluted columns. Beneath the cavetto cornice molding at the top of the trunk is a wide band of scrolled carving flanking the head and shoulders of a man in the center. The door is edge-molded and beneath the shaped top is a motif displaying the entwined letters, JC. In the center of the door is a medallion of the head and shoulders of a man in military dress. Both doors have escutcheon plates. The corners of the trunk and plinth are decorated with quarter-carved columns and the front of the plinth is paneled. The case is supported by ogee bracket feet. Height 97⅝ inches. Painted iron dial with hemispheres and moon phase disc in lunette, and painted figures on the spandrels. The hour and minute hands are pierced and filed and there is a slender sweep seconds hand. The date is shown in a curved aperture, and painted on the dial is the signature Daniel Oyster, Reading. The 8-day brass movement has an anchor escapement and a rack and snail strike system. Another tall case clock by this maker carries a medallion of General Lafayette on the door.

Figure 5.

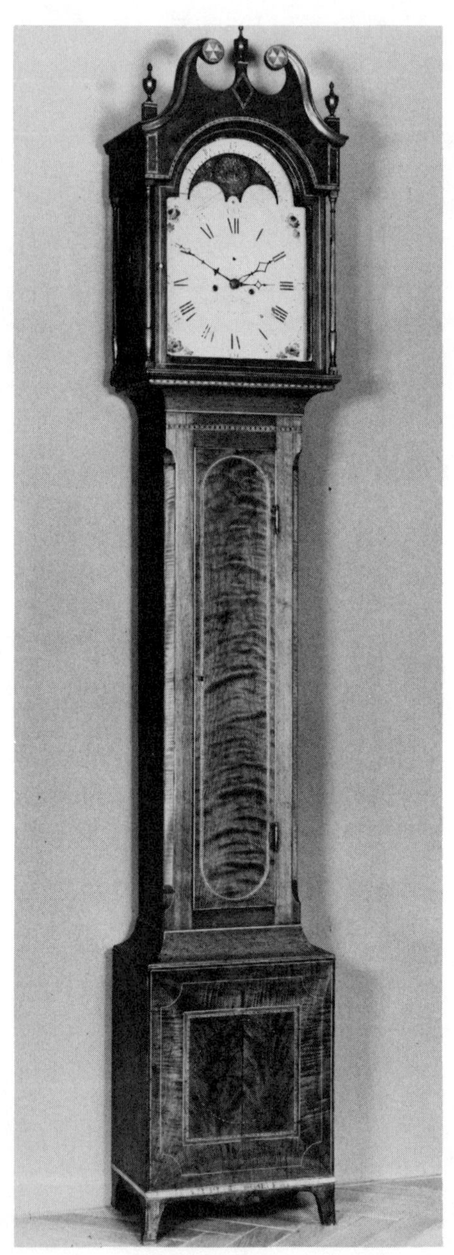

Figure 6.

About 1792 paper dials came into use. They were glued onto metal and wood plates and fitted to the cheapest clocks. By the end of the century the making of brass dials had finished in preference to painted dials, and the use of Arabic numerals was becoming widespread.

Nineteenth century dials continued to be break-arch in shape, but the square portion increased in size, being anything from ten and one-half inches to fourteen and one-half inches.

Many clocks display the phase of the moon through an aperture cut in the lunette. The arrangement consists of a disc, with teeth cut in the rim, that is rotated behind the dial once in every two lunar or moon months. Painted on the disc are two full moons positioned diametrically opposite, and on the arch at the top of the main dial is a scale graduated in twenty-nine and one-half equal divisions. The length of a lunar month is approximately twenty-nine days, twelve hours and forty-five minutes. The bottom edge of the lunette aperture is shaped with two semi-circles, one at each side, which are sometimes painted to

(Left)

Figure 6. 8-day striking tall case clock. Circa 1800. Johnston and Davis, Pittsburgh. The case is walnut with cherry and maple veneer and is decorated with bands of inlay work. The hood pediment is break-arch and carries two scrolls and three turned wood finials. A wood baluster column stands at each corner of the hood and in each side panel is a circular window. At the top and bottom of the trunk is a cavetto molding. The two front corners are chamfered and inlaid and they result at each end in a lamb's tongue. The skirt of the plinth is curved and the case is supported by bracket feet. The copper dial is white enameled and has Roman numerals in the chapter ring and Arabic numerals outside the minute ring. The spandrels are painted with colored flowers, and in the lunette are two hemispheres and a moon phase disc. Behind the moon disc is engraved W. H. Price, Birm'm. and written in ink is For M. Felix Negley. In the upper half of the dial is a subsidiary small seconds dial, and in the lower portion is the signature Johnston and Davis, Pittsburgh. The dial carries a sweep seconds hand, and all hands are pierced and filed. The movement is 8-day brass with striking mechanism. Stamped on the iron plate behind the dial is W. H. Price.

Figure 7.

(Left)

Figure 7. 8-day, mahogany striking tall case clock. Circa 1800 - 1810. William Cummens, Boston or Roxbury, Mass. The case is largely mahogany with mahogany veneer and beading, and satinwood inlay work. The upper break-arch of the hood pediment is formed by a cavetto molding beneath which is an applied fret, and above are three turned brass finials, each standing on a square plinth and separated by a fret. At each corner of the hood stands a turned and kerfed wood column with brass capitals. The upper and lower moldings of the trunk are cavetto. The two front corners have quarter columns matching those of the hood. The inlay and veneer design on the trunk door is repeated on the front of the plinth. Height 98¾ inches. The break-arch dial is white with Roman chapters and Arabic numerals outside the minute ring. The spandrels are painted with flowers and in the lunette are two hemispheres and a moon phase disc. There is a small seconds subsidiary dial and a curved aperture for the date. Painted on the dial is the signature Wm. Cummens. The two main hands are pierced and filed.

(Over Page)

Figure 8. 8-day, mahogany, strike and chime tall case clock. Circa 1800-1816. Maker probably John Hoff or George Hoff, Jr. of Pennsylvania, probably Lancaster. The case is made of mahogany and mahogany veneer on pine with bands of satinwood and ebony inlay work. The top of the break-arch pediment carries two scrolls, two turned brass finials and a brass eagle standing on a ball between the scrolls. At each of the four corners of the hood is a fluted column. At the top and bottom of the trunk is a cavetto molding. The two front corners are chamfered and inlaid and in the center of the door is an inlaid eagle within an oval. The front of the plinth is inlaid complimentary to the trunk door and the front corners are chamfered and inlaid to match the trunk. The skirt of the plinth is serpentine and the clock is supported by curved bracket feet. Height 107 inches. The white painted dial has black Arabic numerals both inside the chapter ring and outside the minute ring. There is a small seconds subsidiary dial and a square date aperture. The center keyhole is for winding the chime. The spandrels are painted with a simple floral design, and the lunette contains two hemispheres and a moon phase disc. The movement is an 8-day strike and chime with an anchor recoil escapement. The clock chimes at each quarter hour. It has 11 bells, 22 hammers and plays 7 tunes.

Figure 8.

represent the east and west hemispheres of the globe. When the disc rotates and the painted moon appears from behind one of the semi-circles, it presents the appearance of a new moon which, as the days move on, gradually comes further into view until it is completely visible, at which stage it represents a full moon. Then, as the disc continues to rotate, the moon slowly disappears behind the other semi-circle until it is out of sight, by which time the other painted moon is ready to appear on the opposite side and begin a new lunar month.

Positioned at the top of each moon is a small pointer adjacent to the graduated scale from which the age of the moon can be read. These moon dials are very popular.

The majority of nineteenth century tall case clocks display some kind of calendar information on the dial. Usually it is the date that can be read through a small square aperture or a curved slot cut in the dial. More expensive clocks were sometimes fitted with dials that carry additional windows through which can be read the name of the day and the name of the month. Most dials were painted with a small subsidiary dial for displaying sceonds. Some makers fitted center sweep seconds hands, but these were not usual.

The number of winding key holes in a dial is an indication of the type of movement that is fitted. One winding hole indicates that there is only a time train to wind. Such a movement is, strictly speaking, a timekeeper and not a clock. Two winding holes are for the time train and a strike train, and if three winding holes are present, the third or center hole is for winding a chime or musical arrangement. When there are no holes at all, winding is accomplished by pulling on the weight line through the trunk door aperture. A clock of this type is usually fitted with a wood movement of one-day or thirty-hour duration that may or may not have a strike train.

Until about 1825 dial hands were individually cut by hand. The delicate work of piercing and filing to shape was carried out by craftsmen who had set themselves up as clock hand makers. It was an expensive operation and about 1825 clockmakers changed to the less costly and more productive method of stamping the hands from thin sheet metal.

Figure 9.

(Left)

Figure 9. 8-day,mahogany and pine, striking tall case clock. Circa 1805. David Shoemaker, Mount Holly, N.J. The hood has a break-arch pediment with a flat top surmounted by two dentiled and inlaid scrolls flanking a gilded wood eagle mounted on a plinth. The plinth is inlaid with 13 stars within an oval, each side of which is a draped fret. The glass door and side windows have break-arch tops. At the top of the hood is a cavetto cornice with dentil molding, and at each corner is a plain turned column. The trunk door has a molded lip edge and a serpentine top, and the keyhole is decorated with ornamental escutcheon. The cornice molding at the top of the trunk is cavetto and that at the base of the trunk is ogee. On the front corners of the trunk and the plinth are fluted quarter columns. The applied panel of the plinth follows the same outline as the trunk door. The design of the feet is ogee bracket. Height 104 inches. The break-arch dial is white enameled and has black Arabic numerals and a subsidiary seconds dial. Pierced and filed hands. Curved aperture for displaying the date. Spandrels are decorated with painted flowers. Hemispheres and a moon phase disc in the lunette. Signature on dial: David Shoemaker, Mount Holly, No. 153. Presented to The Daughters of The American Revolution Museum by Miss Mildred Getty of Maryland. Originally owned by her great great grandfather of Burlington Co., N.J., Joseph Burr to Joshue Shreve Burr to Joseph Franklin Burr.

(Over page)

Figure 10. 8-day, mahogany, striking tall case clock. Circa 1810-1820. George Hagey, Germantown, Pa. The case is mahogany and the front face is mahogany veneer decorated with bands of inlay work and corner fans. The break-arch pediment carries two scrolls and three turned brass finials, each outer finial being mounted on a square fluted plinth. The hood has a fluted column at each front corner and a plain turned column at each rear corner. At the top and bottom of the trunk is a cavetto molding and at each front corner is a fluted quarter column. The clock stands on ogee-bracket feet. Height 95½ inches. The dial has an applied chapter ring and four applied cast brass spandrels reminiscent of eighteenth century English tall case dials. At the bottom of the dial center is a semi-circular date aperture while at the top is a small seconds subsidiary dial. In the lunette is a sailing ship that rocks with the motion of the pendulum. Engraved signature on dial: George Hagey, Germantown. The movement is 8-day and is stamped Osbornes Manufactory, Birmingham: believed to be Birmingham, England.

Figure 10.

In addition to gluing a printed label to the inside of the case trunk, clockmakers invariably had their name and town, and sometimes year of manufacture, painted on the dial.

Dwarf tall case clocks are shortened versions of tall case clocks and are probably better known as grandmother clocks. They stand between three feet, six inches and five feet high. It was quite usual to place them on wall shelves or brackets, and in some instances they resemble Massachusetts shelf clocks.

Dials generally followed the pattern of break-arch, but round and square dials were frequently fitted. Unlike tall case clocks, the addition of calendar work and the provision of a subsidiary dial for seconds was not usual.

Clocks of this type are known to have been made in America as early as 1770, but it was not until 1800 that they were made in any quantity. Their popularity lasted about twenty-five years and by 1830 no more were made.

Movements

Until about 1810 the most usual type of movement fitted to tall case clocks was the eight-day brass with two weights. Other types were thirty-hour brass with endless rope and one driving weight, thirty-hour wood with two weights and dial wind or pull up wind, and eight-day wood with two weights, but this latter movement is rare.

After 1810, the considerably lower priced thirty-hour wood strike movement, mass produced by machine methods in Eli Terry's factory, was on the market and the reduction in cost made it possible for the brass movement to continue on a commercial basis. By 1825 the era for brass movements in tall case clocks was over.

Figure 11.

(Left)

Figure 11. 8-day mahogany, striking, tall case clock. Circa 1810-1820. Jacob Eby, Manheim, Pa. The case is veneered in mahogany and decorated with narrow bands of inlay work. Two inlaid scrolls and three turned brass finials adorn the top of the break-arch pediment. The door has a small brass ornamental drop handle, and at each corner of the hood is a plain turned wood column. The trunk has a cavetto molding at the top and bottom, and the two front corners are chamfered and inlaid. The door has a molded lip edge and the top is shaped. Inlaid above the door is an eagle. The plinth has a serpentine skirt and curved bracket feet. Height 105 inches. The break-arch dial is white with black Arabic numerals. There is a calendar track inside the chapter ring and a seconds track outside. The spandrels are painted with a geometric design and in the lunette are two hemispheres and a moon phase disc. The hands are pierced and filed and are extremely delicate and graceful. The clock has the unusual feature of having a center seconds hand and a center date hand. Signature on dial: Jacob Eby, Manheim. The movement is 8-day and has a dead beat escapement and a rack and snail striking system. Stamped on the false iron plate of the movement is: Patton and Jones, Philadelphia.

(Over page)

Figure 12. 8-day, mahogany, striking tall case clock. Circa 1810-1820. George Jones, Wilmington, Del. The case is made of cherry wood veneered with mahogany and inlaid with satinwood and ebony. The break-arch pediment is surmounted by two scrolls and three brass finials, and is decorated with five-point stars. The frame of the glass break-arch door is inlaid and beaded, and on each side is a fluted column with brass capitals. Two turned wood columns occupy the rear corners of the hood. At the top and bottom of the trunk is a cavetto molding and at each front corner is a fluted quarter column. The top of the door is break-arch in shape and the front is decorated with two rows of inlay work. At the base of the trunk is a panel with a complimentary design of inlay which is repeated on the front face of the plinth. Height 97⅜ inches. The break-arch dial is white enameled and has black Arabic numerals in the chapter and on the outside of the minute track. It has a subsidiary seconds dial and a curved aperture for the date. Pierced and filed hands. The spandrels are painted with figures in pastoral scenes, and in the lunette are two hemispheres and a moon phase disc. Signature on the dial: George Jones, Wilmington, Del. The 8-day brass movement has an anchor recoil escapement and a rack and snail striking system.

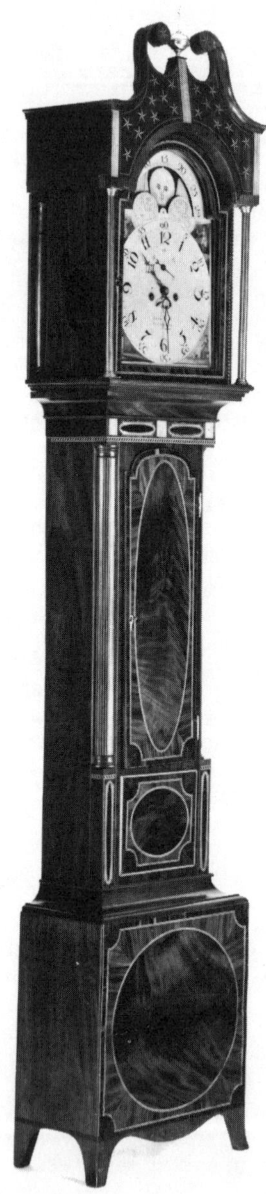

Figure 12.

(Over page)

Figure 13. 8-day, cherry and walnut, striking tall case clock. Circa 1825 - 1834. Humphrey Griffith, Indianapolis, Ind. The break-arch pediment of the hood carries two scrolls and three turned wood finials. Flanking the break-arch glass door are two turned wood baluster columns, and the hood framing at the back has a serpentine profile. At the top and bottom of the trunk is a cavetto molding and the front corners are chamfered terminating at each end in a lamb's tongue. The flat top door is flame veneered and has a molded lip edge. There is a matching rectangular panel beneath. The front of the plinth is plain and has a serpentine skirt and straight bracket feet. Height 99 inches. The break-arch dial is white enameled and has black Arabic numerals and a subsidiary seconds dial. There is a curved aperture for the date. Pierced and filed hands. Painted in the spandrels are shells of many colors. In the lunette are hemispheres and a moon phase disc the decoration of which includes a painted ship. Signature on the dial: H. Griffith, Indianapolis. Presented to The Daughters Of The American Revolution Museum by Mrs. John Newman Carey of Indiana.

(Over page)

Figure 14. 8-day, mahogany, striking dwarf tall case clock. Circa 1815 - 1825. Joshua Wilder, Hingham, Mass. The case is pine and veneered with mahogany. The top of the break-arch hood is decorated with a fret and three turned brass finials mounted on wood pillars. At each side of the break-arch glass door is a tapered plain turned column. The trunk has a cavetto molding at top and bottom, and at each front corner is a plain turned quarter column. The edges of the door are square cut and molded. Ornamental brass hinges are used and a brass escutcheon decorates and protects the keyhole. The skirt of the plinth is serpentine and the case is supported by curved bracket feet. Height 50½ inches. The break-arch dial is white enameled and has black Arabic numerals. The spandrels are painted with an emblem and the break-arch with fruit. Signature on the dial: Jo. Wilder, Hingham. The 8-day brass movement has an anchor escapement, a rack and snail striking system and an 18 inch pendulum.

Figure 13.

Figure 14.

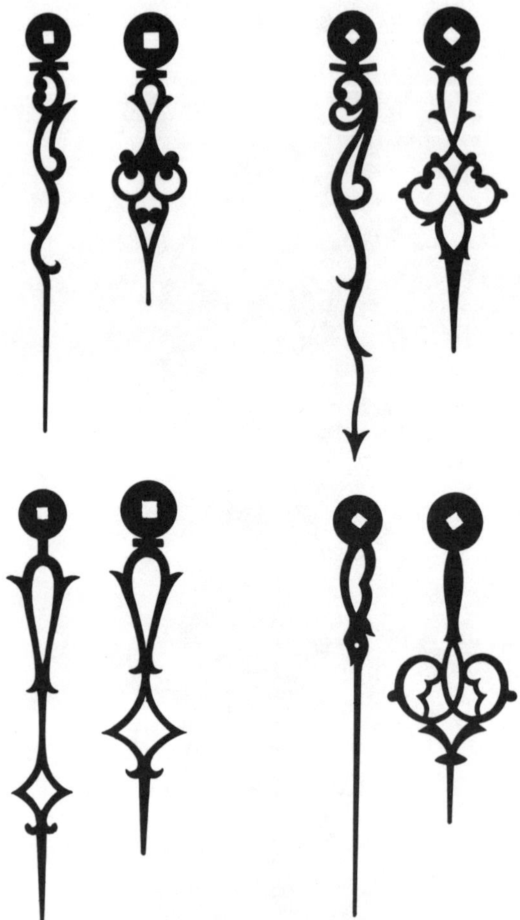

Figure 15. Pre 1825 Hands. Pierced and filed by hand.

(Right)

Figure 16. 8-day, mahogany, striking dwarf tall case clock. Circa 1815 - 1825. Reuben Tower, Plymouth, Hingham and Hanover, Mass. The case is pine and veneered with mahogany. The description of the case is the same as for Fig. 15. Reuben Tower and Joshua Wilder were neighbors and the similarity of the two clock cases might well mean they were made by the same cabinet maker. The break-arch dial is painted white and has black Arabic numerals. Signature on the dial: Reuben Tower. The 8-day brass movement has an anchor escapement, a rack and snail striking system and an 18 inch pendulum.

Figure 16.

CHAPTER 3
Shelf Clocks

Massachusetts

It is thought by many that about 1760 Simon Willard introduced the first American shelf clock. It became known as the Massachusetts shelf clock but is also referred to as half clock, case-on-case and box-on-box. The wood cases frequently possess many of the features and details to be found on tall case clocks, e.g. hood bell tops, frets, finials, break-arch tops, scroll tops, hood columns, side windows, break-arch dials, skirt or molding of the plinth and the shape of the feet, whereas others are plain and not always attractive.

Mahogany and mahogany veneer on pine were the most used woods, but the use of cherry and maple was not unusual. The cases vary in height from about twenty-two inches to approximately forty-four inches. These clocks were popular until about 1830, after which very few were made. When Simon Willard was granted a patent in 1802 for his Improved Timepiece, he discontinued making Massachusetts shelf clocks but his brother Aaron carried on where Simon left off. Between them, the Willards probably made more of this type of clock than any other maker.

Almost all movements are brass with anchor escapements and with running times of two, three or eight days. Very occasionally a movement is found with iron plates and brass bushings for the pivots. It is not uncommon to find some of these clocks fitted with

Figure 17. 2-day cherrywood Massachusetts shelf clock. Circa 1790 - 1810. Attributed to Paul Rogers, Berwick, Me. The case is made of cherrywood and was subsequently painted with floral decoration about 1879. The upper case has a flat top with no decoration and has a break-arch dial opening. The door in the base has a break-arch top. Height 26⅜ inches. In the lunette of the white painted dial are the initials P R, but these have been overpainted with the signature D. Wood. The movement has iron plates and iron plate pillars, while the wheels are made of brass. Arbor pinions run in brass bushings.

Figure 18. 8-day mahogany Massachusetts shelf clock. Circa 1800 - 1810. Aaron Willard, Boston, Mass. The case is made of pine, veneered with mahogany and inlaid with ebony and satinwood. The flat top is surmounted by three finials and a wood fret while the front has a kidney-shaped dial opening. The front of the base is decorated with narrow bands of inlay and corner fans. The skirt is finished with molding and ogee bracket feet. Height 35⁷⁄₁₆ inches. The kidney-shaped dial is painted white and is signed Aaron Willard, Boston. The slender hands and simple design are typical of those so frequently used by Aaron Willard.

Figure 19. Mahogany Massachusetts shelf clock. Circa 1800 - 1815. David Wood, Newburyport, Mass. Mahogany case with narrow bands of inlay work. It has a break-arch dial opening and is surmounted by a single turned metal finial and a wood fret. It is possible that the case originally had three finials. Height 35½ inches. The white painted break-arch dial is signed David Wood.

Figure 20. 8-day mahogany Massachusetts shelf clock. Circa 1810. Nathaniel Munroe, Concord, Mass. The case is made of mahogany with narrow bands of satinwood inlay work. The top is typical of the inverted bell applied to many bracket clocks, the decoration of which is completed by the addition of three turned brass finials and a wood fret. The front is cut away to kidney shape and the lower portion of the glass is reverse painted. The skirt at the bottom is finished with a molding and ogee bracket feet. Height 41 inches. The white painted dial carries the signature N. Munroe. The movement is brass with a strike mechanism for sounding the hours. The wood case behind the movement is stamped W.M.

Figure 21. 8-day mahogany Massachusetts shelf clock. Circa 1810 - 1815. Aaron Willard, Boston, Mass. The case is made of pine, veneered with mahogany and decorated with satinwood inlay work. The flat top with molding is decorated with three metal finials and a wood fret, and the front is cut away for a kidney dial. Height 34 inches. The dial is painted white and at the bottom it carries the signature Aaron Willard, Boston. The hands are typical of those frequently used by Willard.

Figure 22. 2-day mahogany Massachusetts shelf clock. Circa 1815. David Wood, Newburyport, Mass. White pine case veneered with mahogany and inlaid with satinwood and ebony. The plain top has a break-arch pediment with three finials, and a diamond shaped window at each side. The lower case carries a veneered and paneled door inside of which is a paper label printed "David Wood Watch and Clock Maker Newburyport". The label also includes operating instructions. A lion's head ring handle is fitted to each side of the lower case and the front corners are embellished with plain turned quarter columns. Beneath a narrow band of inlay work is a serpentine skirt and in each corner is a curved bracket foot. The clock is supported by a matching wall bracket. Height 33³⁄₁₆ inches. In the lunette of the white painted break-arch dial is a picture of two sailing ships engaged in battle. The movement has a small bell on which the hours are struck.

Figure 23. Mahogany Massachusetts shelf clock. Circa 1818. William Lemist and William B. Tappan, Philadelphia. (Not to be confused with William King Lemist, an apprentice of Simon Willard). The case is made of mahogany and mahogany veneer. Both the door glass and the tablet below are reverse painted. In each spandrel is a lyre decorated with oak leaves and acorns. In the oval beneath is the signature Lemist, Tappan. Philada. within a design of sea shells and flowers. The picture in the tablet below is a near copy of that which can be seen in Fig. 24. Height 38½ inches.

Figure 24. Massachusetts shelf clock. Circa 1820. Aaron Willard, Boston, Mass. Gilded and painted wood case. The flat top is surmounted by a large central pineapple finial and a ball in each corner. The glass surrounding the circular dial, and the tablet below, have both been reverse painted. Immediately below the numeral VI in the black area is a small number that has become obscure, and centrally placed in the lower area is the signature Aaron Willard, Boston. The tablet below portrays a rustic scene with a shepherdess and lamb as the central figures. Note the similarity to the tablet in Fig. 23. The clock stands on gilded cast metal feet. Height 35 inches. The metal dial is white painted and the hands are typical Aaron Willard pattern.

Figure 25. 30-hour cherrywood Massachusetts shelf clock. Circa 1820. Major Timothy Chandler, Concord, N.H. Case is made of cherrywood and red gum stained to resemble mahogany. Flat top hood surmounted by a cast eagle on plinth and flanked by a fret. Plain paneled door, and a serpentine skirt to an otherwise plain plinth. Height 34¾ inches. Square dial with painted spandrels. Signature T. Chandler, Concord. Movement plates are iron, separated by brass pillars. Arbor pivots run in brass bushes.

a rack and snail strike mechanism, and some eighteenth century clocks are known to have alarms.

A distinctive feature of some clocks is the kidney-shaped metal dial, while some circular dials are convex.

Like the tall case clocks, the movements rest on a wood seat board which is supported by two wood brackets screwed to the back of the case. The movement is held to the seat board by screws that pass up through the board and into threaded holes in the bottom plate pillars. The pendulum hangs behind the movement back plate, and the seat board is cut away to allow the pendulum freedom of swing.

Massachusetts shelf clocks were good timekeepers, and their popularity among collectors remains high.

Bracket

Bracket clocks first appeared in England in 1658 and their popularity lasted for two hundred years. They were the first English clocks to be fitted with pendulums and the first to be fitted with movements powered by springs.

In America, bracket clocks first appeared in Boston, Philadelphia, Pennsylvania and Connecticut about 1770 and continued to be made in small quantities until about 1830. The cases were true to English styling but less ornate. There seems to be little doubt that the cases were made in America, but the same cannot be said about the movements. Many think that the movements were imported from England or the parts were shipped over and then assembled. Evidence to support this theory is the appearance on many movements of the names of London makers. Others say that the quality of the springs is superior to any that could have been made in America at that time.

Some clocks have silvered brass dials or dials that have been enameled; these were probably imported. The majority of clocks have hand-painted dials that were produced in America at a much lower cost than could be obtained from England or Europe. Almost all bracket clock dials are painted with the name and town of the maker.

The tops of cases are break-arch or bell-shaped and are fitted

Figure 26. 8-day walnut bracket clock. Circa 1795 - 1810. Thomas Parker, Philadelphia, Pa. The case is made of poplar and veneered with walnut. It has a bell top and break-arch door. Height 19¼ inches. The painted dial is simple and without decoration. In the break-arch is a manually operated hand which enables the owner to select STRIKE or PEACE. These subsidiary dials are now usually marked STRIKE and SILENT. The movement is 8-day brass with a crown wheel and verge escapement and rack and snail strike system. Engraved on the back plate is Thos. Parker, Philadelphia.

Figure 27. 8-day mahogany bracket clock. Circa 1800. Aaron Willard. The bell top case is white pine veneered with mahogany and has a quarter fluted column at each front corner. Painted dial carrying the signature Aaron Willard. Curved calendar aperture. Anchor recoil escapement and rack and snail strike mechanism.

Figure 28. 8-day mahogany bracket clock possibly by Thomas Crow, Wilmington, Delaware. Circa 1805 - 1815. The bell top case is mahogany veneered over pine and inlaid with satinwood. The dial has been repainted and in the break-arch is a circular brass plate engraved Made by Thomas Crow, Wilmington. The combination of a brass nameplate with a painted dial makes documentation questionable. The movement is 8-day brass with a crown wheel and verge escapement and a rack and snail strike system. A mock pendulum is made visible behind a curved aperture in the dial.

with a carrying handle. Turned wood or brass finials are sometimes added to bell tops.

Side panels frequently contain windows of clear glass or they are fretted and backed with colored silk cloth. Frets allow the strike to be heard more clearly.

Cases with bell tops invariably have doors with flat tops, and the spandrels formed by the break-arch are decorated with inlay work, painted designs or thin gilded sheet embossed with a pattern of foliage or silk-backed frets. Ornamental pillars were sometimes fitted to the two front corners.

The case is supported by four feet, usually of wood, shaped to ogee molding, and less frequently of cast metal in the form of a scroll.

The shapes of dials remained true to the English break-arch but American clockmakers introduced their own ideas of decoration. Arabic and Roman numerals were used and, in some instances, both were employed on the same dial; Roman in the chapter to mark the hour positions and Arabic outside the minute ring.

Brass dial plates were silvered, gilded or enameled and dials of wood were hand painted. Subsidiary dials include strike-silent, usually in the lunette, which is pre-set by a manually operated pointer, moon phase, calender aperture, seconds dial and,much less frequently, a mock pendulum. This is a curved slot in the main dial through which can be seen a small piece shaped like a pendulum bob which is attached to the movement pallets. This arrangement provides visual confirmation that the clock is functioning.

The movements are usually brass eight-day spring driven with fusees, rack and snail strike mechanism and calendar work. Similar movements, but weight driven and with anchor escapements, were used in tall case clocks in conjunction with long pendulums. This arrangement responded well to positive and accurate positioning of the clock, but any misalignment of the case or subsequent change of attitude could cause the movement to function out of beat, which invariably resulted in stopping the movement.

This sensitivity does not apply to verge escapements and, because of their portability, bracket clocks were fitted with verge and crown wheel escapements with short half-seconds spring-hung pendulums.

Box Case

In 1810 Eli Terry successfully completed a three-year contract with the Porter brothers to manufacture four thousand thirty-hour wood movements for tall case clocks or hang-up clocks. Shortly after this he sold his premises and retired to a small workshop where he spent much of the next four years designing. He realized that while the low-priced uncased movements he had been making were providing the population with cheap wag-on-wall clocks, they possessed the disadvantages of being unprotected and not being portable.

Terry developed the idea of employing mass production methods to produce inexpensive cased shelf clocks with thirty-hour wood strike movements selling for the incredibly low price of fifteen dollars.

In 1814 Terry began producing a series of experimental clocks, the first of which had plain box-shaped mahogany cases with no form of decoration. These box cases were the forerunners of Terry's famous pillar and scroll clocks, which he introduced in 1818.

In 1816 Terry was granted a patent covering the design of his clock. He later entered into an agreement allowing Seth Thomas to case the movements and sell box case clocks under licence. Meanwhile, Terry continued to develop his ideas.

The first of these box case clocks measured approximately twenty inches high, fourteen inches wide and four inches deep, and they had a flush door closing into a rebate of slightly less dimensions. The door consisted of frame members approximately one and a half inches wide and a single piece of glass to fill the frame. The inside face of the glass was painted with a black circle that filled the upper part of the frame aperture. This represented the dial and inside the circle were reverse painted Arabic numerals. The glass was otherwise clear, making visible the wood movement with its hands, and the bell and pendulum below.

The oak back plate of the movement was made the full width of the case and formed part of the case back. The front plate was an

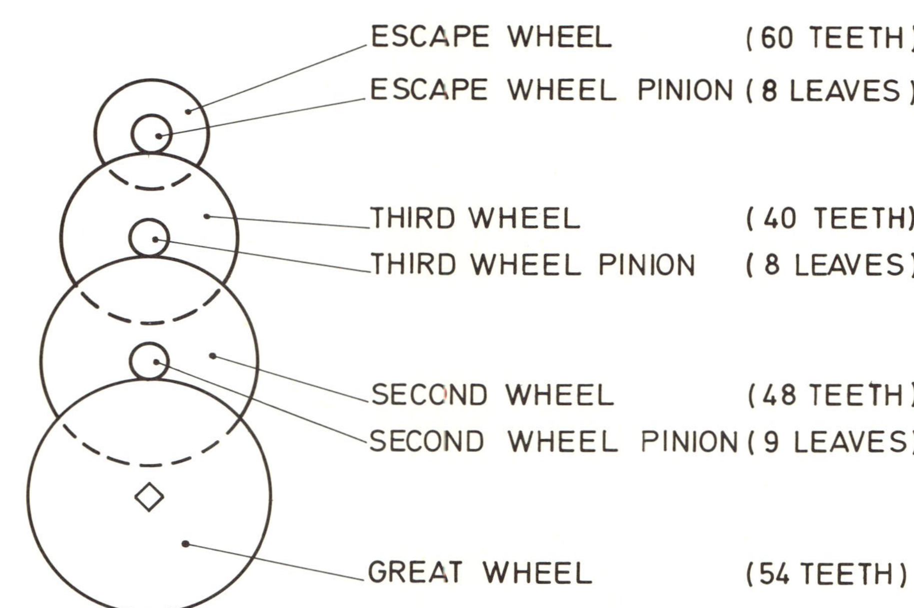

Figure 29. Terry's 30-hour wood, four-wheel, time train.

open frame made of four strips of mahogany. Such a plate is known as a strap plate. Four wood plate pillars were dowelled into the back plate while the front plate was held in position by tapered pins pushed through holes in the front ends of the pillars. Wheels were made of walnut, cherry and mahogany, and apple wood was frequently used for pinions because of its hardness. Arbors or spindles were made of wood with a steel pivot driven into each end.

An entirely original idea of Eli Terry was to transfer the dial motion work from behind the dial to a position between the movement plates. The escapement and pendulum were then brought from the rear of the movement to the front of the strap plate which enabled the movement to be positioned far back inside the case.

The escapement anchor operated on the right-hand side of the escape wheel and was supported by a brass bracket mounted on the strap frame. This bracket also provided an anchorage from which the pendulum was suspended, and its position is the cause of the pendulum hanging off center. The engagement between anchor and escape wheel was adjustable by altering the position of the brass bracket.

The time and strike trains each had four wheels and the strike mechanism was rack and snail. The system employed to suspend the weights is illustrated in Fig. 64(d). The length of the line and the diameter of the drum was such that the movement ran for thirty-two hours. The time train is illustrated in Fig. 29.

Thomas used an oval label bearing the words:

(E. TERRY'S)
Patent Clock
MADE AND SOLD
BY
Seth Thomas
PLYMOUTH CON.

The label was pasted inside the back of the case behind the pendulum bob.

In 1818 Terry redesigned his strap front plate movement to accommodate a wood count wheel; he found it less costly to produce than the brass rack and snail. An example of this movement can be seen in Fig. 32A. That same year an agreement was signed whereby Seth Thomas was able to manufacture these movements under a license. It is believed that Seth Thomas was the only maker to case off-center movements.

A modified version of the original box case clock was made by E. Terry & Sons about 1825. The thirty-hour wood alarm movement and the layout of the case interior are identical to Fig. 33A. It had a white painted square wood dial with black Roman numerals. The door frame included a horizontal bar similar to the doors of pillar and scroll clocks. In the upper opening was a square dial glass while the lower opening was fitted with a reverse painted glass tablet with a central oval of clear glass.

The original box case clocks with the off-center pendulums were made only by Eli Terry and by Seth Thomas.

Pillar and Scroll

In 1818 Eli Terry introduced the pillar and scroll clock but, like the box case clock, the pillar and scroll passed through stages of development before Terry settled with what became recognized as the standard model. The external design was the result of modifying the box case to improve its appearance, and internally the case was modified to accommodate development changes to the thirty-hour wood movement.

Cases were made of solid mahogany and mahogany veneered pine. The top was decorated with a swan neck scroll and three brass finials. At each side of the door was a tall slender turned column, and at the bottom of the case was a serpentine skirt with four straight bracket-type feet.

Terry produced four basic experimental models. The first three had movements with four-wheel trains and the last had a five-wheel train movement. It is the latter that became the standard pillar and scroll clock. For ease of identification it is convenient to refer to them as Model numbers 1, 2, 3 and 4.

Model No. 1 (1818 - 1819)

The door was similar to that of the box case clock in that within its frame it had a single piece of glass but, unlike the box case, the upper portion was left clear through which to see the painted wood dial. The lower portion was reverse painted with a central

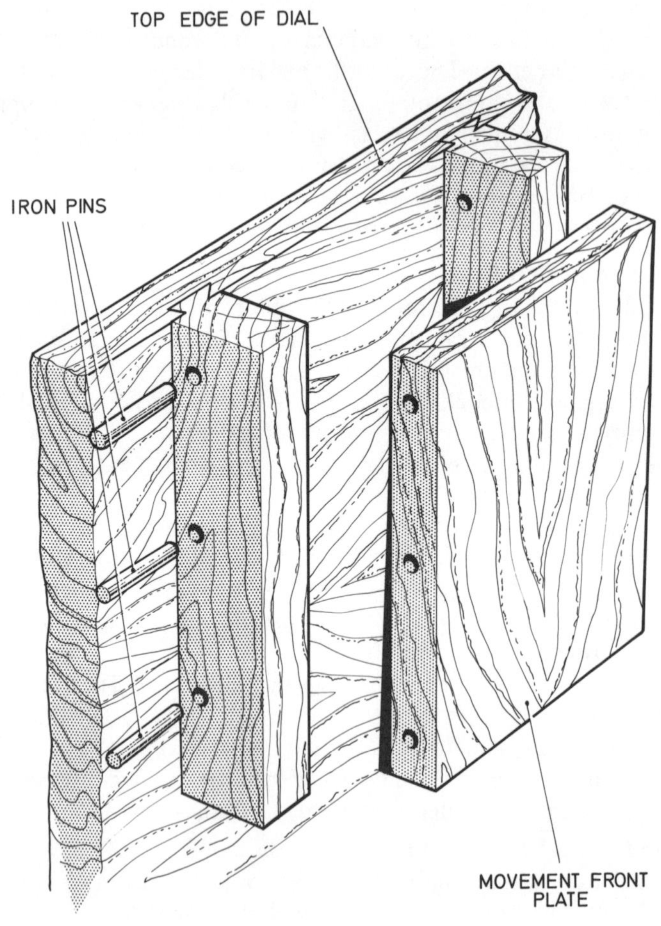

Figure 30. Early Terry pillar and scroll dial fixing.

oval of clear glass for keeping the pendulum bob visible.

Inside the case there were no partitions. The clock label on the lower portion of the case back bore the words:

PATENT
Made and Sold by
ELI TERRY
Plymouth
CON.

All but the word PATENT were enclosed within an oval.

The dial was white painted wood with black Arabic numerals and minute ring. The spandrels were decorated with color, usually floral or foliage designs. The movement was held to the dial by pins, Fig. 30. Two vertical wood members were dovetailed into the rear face of the dial at a distance sufficient to allow the movement front plate to enter between them. Three holes were drilled in each member and steel pins passed through these holes and into the thickness of the movement front plate.

The thirty-hour wood movement had two solid plates, the back plate being the full width of the case and forming part of the case back like box case clocks. The front plate was rectangular, being wider than it was high. It was held to the plate pillars by tapered pins that passed through the projecting front ends of the pillars.

The time and strike trains each had four wheels, the ratios being the same as those for box case clocks.

The strike was controlled by a rack and snail, and the mechanism was positioned in front of the front plate.

The escape wheel, anchor, crutch and upper half of the central pendulum were visible in front of the dial. This arrangement has become known as Terry's outside escapement. The lower half of the pendulum rod is hidden from view behind the tablet, but the pendulum bob can be seen through the oval of clear glass.

The line arrangement for carrying the weights is the same as for box case clocks, i.e. Fig 64 (d).

Model No. 2 (1819)

The differences are in the design of the door and the method of controlling the strike.

Figure 31. 30-hour mahogany pillar and scroll clock. Circa 1822. Eli Terry, Plymouth, Connecticut. Swan neck scroll top with 3 brass finials. Reverse painted tablet of Mount Vernon. The position of the clear glass oval indicates a centrally hung pendulum. Clock paper reads: "Patent Clocks,/ made and sold at Plymouth Conn./ by/ Eli Terry/ inventor and patentee". Height 28 inches. Width 15⅜ inches. Depth 4 inches.

Terry introduced a horizontal dividing strip of wood into the door frame thereby creating two apertures and the need for two pieces of glass. The upper glass was square to conform to the shape of the dial, while the lower glass became an independent tablet.

The strike mechanism was changed to count wheel which was positioned centrally in front of the movement front plate. Terry found that this method of strike control was quicker and cheaper to produce.

Model No. 3 (1819)

In this model Terry changed the position of the escapement and slightly altered his clock label.

The escapement and pendulum assembly were transferred from the front of the dial and repositioned immediately behind the dial plate. This arrangement is known among collectors as Terry's inside-outside escapement.

To the clock label was added the word INVENTED which was placed above the original wording within the oval.

Model No. 4 (1822)

After the introduction of Model No. 3 Terry began experimenting with thirty-hour wood movements with trains of five wheels and, at the same time, he modified the case interior. Early in 1822 he introduced his final model, which was an immediate success and became America's first mass-produced shelf clock.

Terry was granted a patent for this improved clock in 1823 but despite this precaution, many other makers copied his clock, avoiding infringement of patent by making changes to the design of the movement. It seems evident that either Terry did not seek legal advice in the preparation of his specification, or if he did, the advice was inadequate. Inevitably there are numerous variants, but it is Terry's clock with the five-wheel train movement that is considered the standard pillar and scroll.

Figs. 33 and 33A are those of a later clock but they serve to illustrate the internal design of the case and the appearance of the movement. Two full height partitions were fitted inside to create

Figure 32. 30-hour mahogany pillar and scroll clock. Circa 1824. Seth Thomas, Plymouth, Connecticut. Swan neck scroll top with 3 brass finials. Reverse painted tablet with off center clear oval glass.

Figure 32A. Door open and hands and dial removed exposing Eli Terry 30-hour strap plate movement with count wheel strike mechanism and off center pendulum. Full width clock label reads: "Patent Clocks,/ Made and sold by/ Seth Thomas."

Figure 33. 30-hour mahogany pillar and scroll alarm clock. Circa 1827. Eli Terry, Plymouth, Connecticut. Swan neck scroll top with 3 brass finials. Reverse painted tablet of Mount Vernon. The position of the clear glass oval indicates a centrally hung pendulum as seen in Fig. 33A. The alarm set disc is in the center of the dial beneath the hands.

Figure 33A. Door open and hands, alarm disc and dial removed. The alarm disc and cam have been placed in the bottom right-hand corner. 30-hour, solid plate wood movement with count wheel strike mechanism. Anchor beneath escape wheel allowing pendulum to hang centrally. The crown wheel and verge alarm mechanism can be seen bottom center.

self-contained compartments for the weights and movement.

The height of the movement plates was increased to accommodate the extra wheels and while the back plate still formed part of the case back it was no longer cut to the width of the case. It was the same size as the front plate. The back plate was protected on the outside by a piece of tinned iron sheet.

The pin on which the escapement anchor pivoted was part of a bush which was a friction fit in the front plate. The pin was off center and by turning the bush the position of the anchor could be adjusted in relation to the escape wheel. The gear ration of the five wheel time train is illustrated in Fig. 34.

The addition of an extra wheel to the two trains meant that the movement could run for thirty hours with a shorter weight line than was required for the earlier four-wheel train movements. Terry increased the height of the case, he positioned the top pulley higher into the roof, and he tied the outer ends of the lines directly to the weights instead of returning the lines to the top of the case. This arrangement is illustrated in Fig. 64(b). The poundage for each weight was approximately 3 lbs 10 oz.

With the introduction of this new clock Terry enlarged his clock label to take up the full width of the case. The wording in the center compartment read as follows:

Patent Clocks
MADE AND SOLD AT PLYMOUTH, CON.
BY
Eli Terry,
INVENTOR AND PATENTEE
WARRANTED IF WELL USED

N.B. The public may be assured that this
kind of Clock will run as long without repairs,
and be as durable and accurate for keeping time,
as any kind of Common Clock whatever.

The words Patent Clocks were printed with old English upper and lower case type, while a more modern upper and lower case was used for printing the name Eli Terry. The style lasted but a short time and when the labels were reprinted a script upper and lower case type was used for the words Patent Clocks, the name Eli Terry was printed in capitals and the word Common was omitted. Wording of left hand label:

DIRECTIONS
TO SET THIS CLOCK RUNNING

Make the Clock fast where it is to stand, exactly in a perpendicular position, and take off the hands and face. The face can be taken off by drawing two pins from a piece below it, and pulling it forward by the lower side.

Oil the pivot on which the brass wheel turns, the pallets or ends of the part commonly called the verge, the pin on which the verge plays, and the wire which carries the pendulum at the place where it touches the rod. A drop of oil is sufficient for the whole, if rightly applied. The pendulum should be put on with the hook towards you. The end of each cord must be tied to the ring at the top of the weight. Care should be taken not to suffer the key to be put on and turned until the cord is on the pulley at the top of the case, and the weights put on. It is immaterial whether the Clock is wound up and put in motion before or after the face and hands are put on.

Wording of right hand label:

DIRECTIONS,
TO KEEP THIS CLOCK IN ORDER.

To wind up the weights, put on the key with the handle or crank downwards, turn towards the 6 o'clock figure, and keep steady turning until the weight is up, then ease back and take off the key.

If the hands want moving, do it by means of the longest, turning at any time forward but never backwards when the Clock is within 15 minutes of striking, nor further than to carry the longest hand up to figure XII.

If the Clock should strike wrong in consequence of its having run down, or other accident, it may be made to strike until it comes to the right hour, by means of a wire below the face directly under the 7 o'clock figure. - The most convenient way of doing it, is to take the key, put the handle in the ring, pull downwards lightly, and as soon as you perceive the work moving, take away the key, and when it has done striking, repeat the operation if necessary, until it comes to the right hour.

At about the time when Terry produced Model No. 1, Seth Thomas began converting box cases into pillar and scroll cases and fitting Terry's thirty-hour four-wheel strap plate movements with count wheel strike and off-center pendulum.

About 1826 Terry introduced an alarm mechanism, an

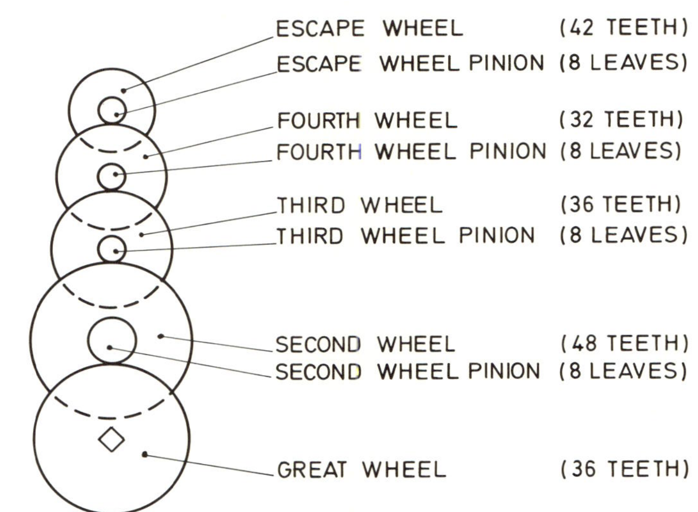

Figure 34. Terry's 30-hour wood, five wheel time train.

example of which can be seen in Fig. 33A. Mounted horizontally on the floor of the case is a length of tube with a ratchet wheel and pawl at the right-hand end and a crown wheel and verge at the opposite end.

Around the tube is wound a full length spiral wire spring, one end of which is fixed to the ratchet wheel while the other end is anchored to the crown wheel.

Attached to the verge is a vertical hammer shaft with its head operating inside a dome bell screwed to the back of the case.

The hammer head is held in place by the lower end of a vertical alarm rod with a central pivot. The upper end is in contact with a tubular cam attached to the rear of the alarm setting disc.

To set the alarm the ratchet wheel is rotated manually until the coil spring is fully wound, and the graduated alarm disc is turned manually to the hour required.

The tubular cam of the setting disc is a friction fit over the hour hand tube and therefore rotates with the hour hand. When the cam reaches its predetermined position the upper end of the alarm rod drops into the cutaway portion of the cam, causing the lower end of the alarm rod to move clear of the hammer head.

The energy in the coiled spring activates the crown wheel and verge causing the hammer to oscillate and sound the bell.

Shortly after Terry introduced the five-wheel train pillar and scroll clock, Seth Thomas began making them despite the fact that there was no agreement with Terry giving him the right. In 1827 Terry started legal proceedings against him but subsequently withdrew the charges apparently on the grounds that there had been no infringement of patent.

Other makers were quick to seize the opportunity and they followed the example of others who had been less cautious and were already producing modified versions of the original. The production of wood movement shelf clocks became widespread. This was the beginning of the American industry of mass produced shelf clocks.

The five-wheel train pillar and scroll first made by Seth Thomas carried an oval clock label bearing the words:

(E. TERRY'S)
Patent Clock
MADE AND SOLD
BY
Seth Thomas
PLYMOUTH CON.

but subsequent clocks had a more detailed label as shown in Fig. 32A.

Pillar and scroll clocks continued to be made during the remaining years of the nineteenth century by different makers. Thirty-hour wood movements, some with roller pinions, were being fitted up to at least 1840; after that the movements were generally eight-day brass.

Pillar and Scroll Looking Glass

From 1818 to about 1825 there were a number of variants of pillar and scroll clocks with a looking glass in the lower portion of the door. These clocks were fitted with Joseph Ives thirty-hour wood movements with iron roller pinions.

The first of these clocks were produced by the firm Ives & Lewis. The outward appearance of the case was similar to but taller than those made by Eli Terry or Seth Thomas, but inside there were no partitions separating the weights and lines from the pendulum. The movement plates were made of mahogany instead of the usual oak, and special care was taken with the turning and finish of the plate pillars.

The dial was eight inches square and secured to four pillars on the front plate by pins. The escapement was positioned between the plates and a short half seconds pendulum was used. The arrangement for the weight lines was as shown in Fig 64(b).

About three years later the same firm introduced another variant. The case had a solid flat base and no internal partitions. The door was hung across the full width of the case and carried a reeded column down each side. Below the looking glass, but still within the door frame, was a small reverse painted glass tablet with a clear oval in the center in line with the path of the pendulum bob. The size of the square dial was increased to twelve inches. The anchor escapement was positioned on the outside of the front plate, and a pendulum approximately twenty-five inches long was used. The slower action resulting from the longer pendulum provided greater latitude for regulation in timekeeping. The line arrangement remained the same as for the previous variant.

The Jerome firms and the firm of Merriman, Birge & Co., all made pillar and scroll looking glass clocks. The cases were similar to the clock previously mentioned. Merriman, Birge & Co. dispensed with line pulleys allowing the weights to hang directly from the movement drums. To prevent the lines interfering with the long pendulum, a vertical partition was placed across the full width of the case behind the pendulum and in front of the lines. The clocks made by the Jerome firms had line arrangements as used by Ives & Lewis.

The dome-shaped strike bell of the earliest of these clocks was secured to the back of the case immediately below the movement. Bells of later clocks were positioned outside the case, on top behind the splat, and a slot was cut in the roof through which the hammer operated. These movements with overhead strike became known as groaners because of the noise made by the meshing gears during striking.

The popularity of these clocks was surpassed in 1825 by the bronze looking glass case.

Bronze Looking Glass

In 1827 Chauncey Jerome introduced the bronze looking glass clock. He was probably influenced by the growing demand for painted furniture that was fashionable at the time.

The case was similar in size and general layout to that of the pillar and scroll looking glass case except that the top carried a splat instead of a swan neck scroll and finials, and at each side of the door was a broad half-round column. The most popular designs for the splat were bowls of fruit and eagles. The splat and columns were painted black and the designs were stencilled by applying bronze powder. The use of a metallic powder in the form of a bronze pigment was cheaper than using gold leaf.

The first of these clocks was fitted with a thirty-hour wood movement designed and made by Chauncey Jerome's youngest brother, Noble. The pendulum length was 17.35 inches. While these movements functioned well, they were non-standard and as such were more costly to produce.

In 1828 Chauncey Jerome changed to Terry's thirty-hour, five train movements, but to avoid infringement of patent rights, he fitted escape wheels with thirty-two teeth instead of the forty-two teeth used by Terry. The effect was to alter the pendulum length from 8.9 inches to 15.4 inches. These changes were enough to prevent any legal action being taken by Eli Terry and at the same time enabled Jerome to use a movement that was readily available at a competitive price. In this respect other makers followed Jerome's lead and the modified Terry movement became a popular choice.

Lighthouse

Simon Willard introduced what he called his lighthouse clock and obtained a patent covering the design in 1822. The general shape resembled that of the Eddystone lighthouse at Plymouth, England, and the clock is frequently referred to by that name. While many collectors may now regard the design as pleasing in appearance, these clocks were not popular when they were first introduced and so very few were made; consequently they are extremely rare.

The wood cases are mahogany, some of which carry brass ornaments. The upper half is circular and slightly tapered, while the lower half can be square, round or octagonal, and is supported by four feet usually spherical. The circular flat top on which the movement is mounted is cut away to provide a slot in which the pendulum rod may swing, and a hole through which the weight line may pass. The height of these clocks varies from about twenty-three inches to approximately thirty-two inches.

The movements are brass eight-day with dead beat anchor escapements. Usually they are fitted with alarm or strike, and the

Figure 35. Mahogany 8-day lighthouse alarm clock. Circa 1822. Simon Willard, Roxbury, Mass. The round trunk is mounted on an octagonal base and is supported by four spherical feet. Height 29¾ inches.

bell is mounted above the dial. Those with alarm mechanisms have an alarm set disc which is rotated manually in the center of the dial. Winding is done by a key, the squared winding arbor being projected forward immediately beneath the dial rim.
bell is mounted above the dial. Those with alrm mechanisms have an alarm set disc which is rotated manually in the center of the dial. Winding is done by a key, the squared winding arbor being projected forward immediately beneath the dial rim.

Dials are engraved brass or white porcelain and carry the signature of Simon Willard. They and their movements are protected from dirt and dust by a glass dome.

Carved Column and Stenciled Column

In 1828 George Mitchell engaged Elias Ingraham to design a shelf clock case in competition with Chauncey Jerome's successful bronze looking glass clock. From these efforts a case with carved splat, columns and lions' paw feet was produced into which Mitchell fitted wood movements made by Ephraim Downs. The cases were usually made of mahogany and mahogany veneered pine, and were anything from twenty-four to about forty-onc inches in height. The sides were tenoned into the base and into the top of the case, and the two front corners each carried a quarter-round, a half-round or flat column. Above each column was a square plinth, frequently surmounted by a finial, and between the two plinths was a splat. Popular finials were the pineapple shape and turned wood.

On the front of the case was a single door which was usually hinged on the right, but some cases are known where the doors are hinged on the left. The door is divided by a horizontal wood member to form two frames.

Decoration of the case was achieved by carving or stenciling. Bowls of fruit and eagles are two designs that were regularly carved or stenciled on the shaped splats, and almost all side columns were carved or stenciled.

The door frames were veneered and invariably fitted with a lock. The upper half of the door carried a square dial glass while in the lower area was a reverse painted glass tablet of a landscape or well known building. Both pieces of glass were held to the door frame by putty. When painting the glass tablet an oval of clear glass was retained through which the bob of the pendulum could be observed.

It was not unusual to use gold leaf on some cases as an additional means of decoration. A number of clocks are known where this has been applied to the carving on the splat and on the side columns.

Many cases do not have feet, their flat base rests directly on the shelf, but where feet have been fitted they usually take the form of balls or carved lions' paws at the front and turned feet at the rear.

Then came the double-decker case with two doors at the front. The external design was such as to create the impression of two sections mounted one upon the other.

All movements were weight driven. Makers used thirty-hour and eight-day wood, including the horizontal Torrington type, and eight-day brass, but it was the thirty-hour wood that was most generally used. Among the eight-day brass were strap movements with roller pinions. Wood movements were fitted with count wheel strikes, whereas brass movements had rack and snail mechanisms. Clocks with alarm mechanisms are not uncommon. Strikes were made on bells or wire gongs or both.

Generally, the methods used to secure the movements in their cases were very similar to the installations found in pillar and scroll clocks. The arrangements for weights, lines and pulleys was as shown in Fig. 64(d). Slots were cut in the roof of the case through which protruded the upper pulleys. Small blocks of wood were sometimes fitted over these slots to act as dust covers.

Dials were white with black Roman or Arabic numerals. Sometimes they carried a small seconds subsidiary dial. The dial plates were square, measuring from four and one-half inches to about six inches.

Then, in 1831, Elias Ingraham designed the triple deck case.

Transition

About 1830 a short pendulum shelf clock with wood movement appeared that bore a marked resemblance to both the pillar and scroll clock and the stenciled or carved column clock. Features of

Figure 36. Mahogany 8-day carved column shelf clock. Circa 1830. Carved half round columns and carved splat with bowl of fruit. Turned mahogany finials. A narrow tablet, 2¼ inches x 10¼ inches, ornamented with a gold eagle and 13 stars, separates the dial glass from the lower glass tablet. The tablet measures 15½ inches high x 10¼ inches wide and is reverse painted with Mount Vernon in landscape enclosed with a floral band of gold on black. Carved paw feet. Height 41 inches. Width 17½ inches. Square white dial with black Roman numerals and floral design in center and in spandrels. Eagles on both hands. Eli Terry 8-day wood movement with strike. Clock paper: "Eight day clock with the improvement of Ivory Bushings, manufactured and sold by Marsh Gilbert & Company, Farmington, Conn".

both types of cases formed part of the design. The scroll top, the slender turned side columns and the distinctive serpentine base of the pillar and scroll were used with the stenciled or carved splat, the half or quarter columns and the paw feet of the carved column clock in any combination. Sometimes the splat was cast from plaster of Paris to resemble carving, and finished in gold leaf.

Ogee (O.G.)

In 1837 America suffered a major financial depression and the clock industry was badly affected. There was a period when very few clocks were made, and many makers were forced out of business. Before the depression the majority of clocks had wood movements which of necessity had to be larger than a corresponding movement made of brass, and the size of the case was partially influenced by the size of the movement.

Business for Chauncey Jerome was as bad as for any clockmaker, but one night during the depression he had an idea. Clocks were an essential part of life and if they could be made cheap enough people would buy. He engaged his young brother Noble who designed a low cost thirty-hour rolled brass movement with count wheel strike. Chauncey Jerome fitted these movements into small simple cases framed in O.G. molding, and a new type of clock was introduced.

Success was immediate and eventually there were more of these clocks being sold than any other Connecticut shelf clock. A new company was formed to handle them and the clock papers announced the manufacturer as JEROMES, GILBERT, GRANT & CO., Bristol, Conn.

As was usual under such circumstances, other makers followed Jerome's example and the manufacture of wood movements began to decline.

In 1842 Jerome shipped to England the first of many consignments of his cheap thirty-hour brass clocks. This was the beginning of America's clock export business.

The case was rectangular with all sides flat. There were no feet. The front carried a wide frame of S-shaped molding known as O.G. and within the frame was the door. The cases were made of pine which was usually veneered with mahogany, but rosewood

Figure 37. Mahogany 30-hour carved column shelf clock. Circa 1830 - 1832. Carved half round columns and carved splat with eagle. Turned mahogany finials. The glass tablet measures 10½ inches high x 10¾ inches wide and is reverse painted with Arlington Mansion in landscape enclosed within a black border with a gold floral design. Carved paw feet. Height 32 inches. Width 17 inches. Square white dial with black Arabic numerals with a floral design in the center and gold spandrels. Eli Terry 30-hour wood movement with strike. Clock paper: "Modern Improved Clocks made and sold by Riley Whiting, Winchester, and cased by Wm. A. Whiting & Co., Buffalo, New York."

Figure 38. Mahogany triple deck case by Barnes, Bartholomew & Co. Circa 1832. The center and bottom panels are reverse painted glass tablets. The bottom tablet has an oval of clear glass indicating the movement has a long pendulum. The side pillars are part gilded and supported by carved paw feet. The height to the top of the carved eagle is 37 inches and the width is 17 inches.

veneer was not unusual. The flat door had two apertures. At the top was the square dial opening while beneath was a glass tablet or, less frequently, a mirror. The glass tablet was reverse painted with a pictorial or landscape scene, a building, animals or floral design, or it could be etched with a geometric pattern. The majority of doors were fitted with a lock.

Evidence of the popularity of O.G. clocks is the demand which continued until 1914. After that date manufacture came to an end. The most usual types made were:

19 inches: 30-hour brass weight driven
26 inches: 30-hour wood 〃 〃
26 inches: 30-hour brass 〃 〃
34 inches: 8-day brass 〃 〃
16 inches: 30-hour brass spring 〃
18 inches: 30-hour brass 〃 〃
18 inches: 8-day brass 〃 〃

but always the thirty-hour brass movement was the favorite.

Previously, plates and wheels of brass movements had been cast which required considerable time being spent on their dressing and polishing. Noble Jerome revolutionized this process by using stampings from rolled brass sheet. The result was a cheaper, lighter and better looking product that could be made more easily and in less time. Contrary to common belief the reduced thickness of the plates and wheels appeared not to have any adverse effect on the running of the movement. Noble Jerome created a further saving by fitting a count wheel strike mechanism in place of the more usual rack and snail. It was cheaper to produce.

The arrangement of the weight line was as shown in Fig. 64(d). Some later clocks were fitted with alarm, the mechanism being separate from the movement and mounted on the case back below the movement. The alarm setting disc was fitted in the center of the dial.

Other makers adopted the same basic idea but introduced their own design of thirty-hour brass movements and alarm mechanisms.

Dials were usually square, about four and one quarter inches, painted white with black Roman numerals. Frequently they were made with a circular aperture at the center exposing the escape wheel and pallets.

Seth Thomas was among the many makers of O.G. clocks which can frequently be instantly recognized by the use of his own unique design of hands. The minute hand was shaped with a letter S on its shank while the hour hand carried a letter T.

Kitchen

During the period from 1840 - 1880 Connecticut makers produced small, low-priced wood timepieces with alarm for use in kitchens. The cases were usually made of pine, rosewood or mahogany. Doors were frequently veneered and carried a glass tablet in the lower half. The height of these clocks varied from about nine to twelve inches and had flat, round or three or four sided tops.

Movements were usually thirty-hour brass spring driven with built in alarm mechanism. Some clocks had eight-day movements with strike. Dials were round or square and painted white with black Roman numerals.

Large quantities of these clocks were made which makes them not too difficult to find, and they are popular among collectors.

Beehive

The beehive clock has the distinction of being the first American production clock to be powered by coil springs. As such it was the pioneer of a new phase in clockmaking which, in the space of a few years, replaced the demand for weight driven clocks.

The classical name is Round Gothic because of its similarity to Gothic arches with their curved and pointed tops. It is also known as the beehive clock, presumably because the shape is reminiscent of old style beehives. Cases of the same shape were also made in England early in the 1820's and were known as lancet cases.

Beehive clocks were introduced by Ray & Ingraham (Andrew) in 1841 and were made by Elisha Curtis Brewster. Their popularity spread and many other makers became involved in their manufacture which continued until the early years of the twentieth century.

Figure 39. Rosewood 8-day kitchen clock. Circa 1880. Seth Thomas Clock Co., on dial.

The general design of the case can be seen in Fig. 40. Half-round molding was used for the sides and arch, and tablet and dial frames, and the case was finished with mahogany or rosewood veneer. Another popular form of decoration is known as ripple. Instead of using half-round molding, flat pieces were used which were impressed with a ripple design by being passed through patterned metal rollers or by pressure from dies.

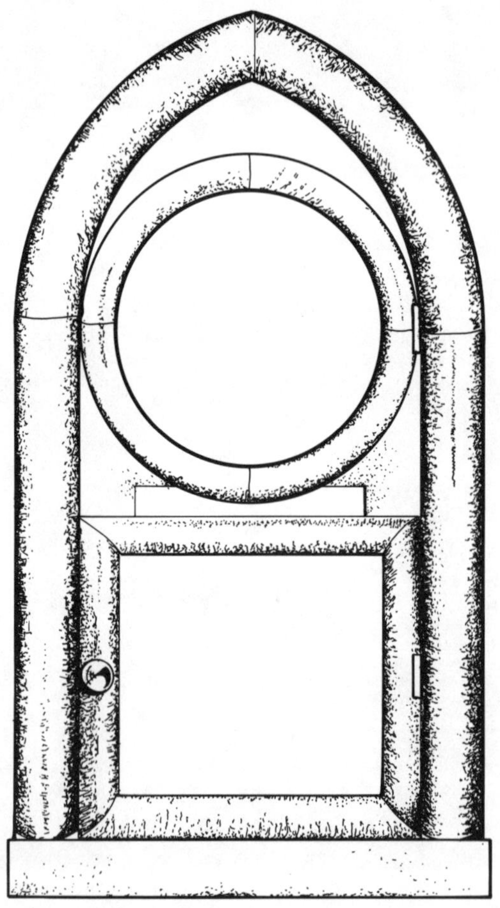

Figure 40. Outline of typical beehive case.

The square glass tablet beneath the dial was usually decorated with a design produced by acid etching, sometimes referred to as frosting. The glass was coated with a thin film of wax and the design was scribed in the wax. Acid was applied to the plate and surface corrosion took place only where the glass was exposed. It was more usual to etch the background and leave the design in clear glass. The wood frame for the tablet and that for the dial glass were made as one and as such formed the door.

The height of these clocks varied between eighteen and twenty inches, while the width was about eleven inches and the depth approximately four inches. Some miniature clocks were made but they were fitted with thirty-hour movements.

The first beehive clocks to be made by E.C. Brewster had eight-day brass strike movements powered by brass springs with brass reverse fusees and cast iron spring housings, the spring fusee unit being screwed to the bottom of the case. The process of making brass springs was covered by a patent granted to J.S. Ives in 1836.

The dials were white painted iron and carried the signature E.C. Brewster, Bristol, Ct. The strike hammer operated against a coiled iron gong secured to the back of the case immediately below the movement. The case had no clock label.

In 1843, E.C. Brewster fitted Kirk patent eight-day movements. In that year Charles Kirk patented a new type of spring driven eight-day brass movement with modified rack and snail strike mechanism. The back plate was made of cast iron and part of the casting consisted of two wells in which to house the two brass springs. Kirk dispensed with the use of fusees by attaching the mainspring direct to the great wheel arbor.

Screwed to the back of the case, beneath the movement, was a thick ornamental cast iron lyre-shaped pierced plate to which the strike gong was attached. The label in these clocks read:

E.C. BREWSTER & Co.,
MANUFACTURERS OF
PATENT SPRING
EIGHT-DAY REPEATING
BRASS CLOCKS
BRISTOL, CONN.

It was not long after the Kirk patent eight-day cast iron movements were first fitted that E.C. Brewster introduced a thirty-hour movement with the same cast iron back plate but with a count wheel strike mechanism. E.C. Brewster also supplied these eight-day and thirty-hour movements to other makers and they were therefore also fitted to other types of shelf clocks under their respective makers' names.

Throughout the remaining years of the nineteenth century the design of the early cases continued with little change. Mechanisms varied slightly. Some makers introduced alarm. These carried a setting disc in the center of the dial, and screwed to the back of the case beneath the movement was a small spring powered hammer mechanism that was released by the clock movement through a vertical wire. In some installations the alarm hammer had its own bell while other makers fitted a bell that was common to strike and alarm.

Not all makers used Kirk's patent cast iron movement. The popularity of the fusee continued but the spring fusee units were attached to the bottom of the movement plates instead of the original position in the bottom of the case.

Crane Patent Year Clock

Aaron Dodd Crane invented the torsion or rotary pendulum brass movement with count wheel strike. Instead of the conventional swinging pendulum with its rod and bob weight, Crane used a long thin ribbon of steel, about eleven inches long, at the end of which was suspended a heavy ball. After setting the movement in motion by rotating the ball in a horizontal plane, the subsequent twisting and untwisting motion of the steel ribbon actuated pawl levers which controlled the release of the escape wheel, which in turn imparted an impulse to the steel ribbon. The effect was to provide long vibrations of a slow rate which resulted in a considerably extended duration.

The original design included a pendulum with a single large ball and was covered by a patent in 1841. Fourteen years later, in 1855, Crane was granted another patent that covered movements with pendulums carrying two or more balls. These balls were usually made of lead encased in brass.

Year clocks were powered by strong springs with fusees and ran for almost four-hundred days, but they must not be confused with the more modern German 400-day clocks.

Crane year clocks continued to be made until 1860 but the single large ball of the pendulum was replaced by three or six small balls. The movement was regulated by moving these balls closer to or further from the center by screw adjustment.

In the meantime, eight-day and one-month movements were produced using the same type of pendulum and escapement as the year clocks but driven by weights. Unlike other weight driven clocks, Crane's movements had less friction to overcome and so considerably lighter weights were used.

A torsion pendulum with six lead balls weighs about three and one quarter pounds.

Movements were usually fitted into mahogany veneered Empire style cases with two or four large diameter wood columns, or bevel cases similar in design to the O.G. case but using a flat molding. Cases measured approximately twenty-one inches high. From 1849 on, Crane fitted his movements into a variety of cases but usually they were not repeated.

The firm of J.R. Mills & Co., which later became The Year Clock Co., made these clocks for Crane, and when The Year Clock Co. went out of business in 1848 Crane continued on his own, assisted by his son Moses, until he died in 1860.

Details are as follows:

1841 - 1843	James R. Mills, Belleville, N.J. on clock paper and dial
1844 - 1845	J.R. Mills & Co., 109 Fulton Street N.Y. on clock paper
1846 - 1848	The Year Clock Co., 35 Cortland St. N.Y. on clock paper
1849 - 1857	Crane, 6 Lombardy St. Newark, N.J.
1858 - 1860	Crane & Son, Boston, Mass.

A few other firms made torsion pendulum clocks under licence but not in large numbers.

When The Year Clock Co. took over from J.R. Mills & Co.,

they used existing stocks of dials that carried the name James R. Mills & Company.

Hour Glass

About 1841 Joseph Ives introduced a type of clock that resembled an hour glass or egg timer in shape. The curves of the frame were achieved by the use of wood laminations, the finished

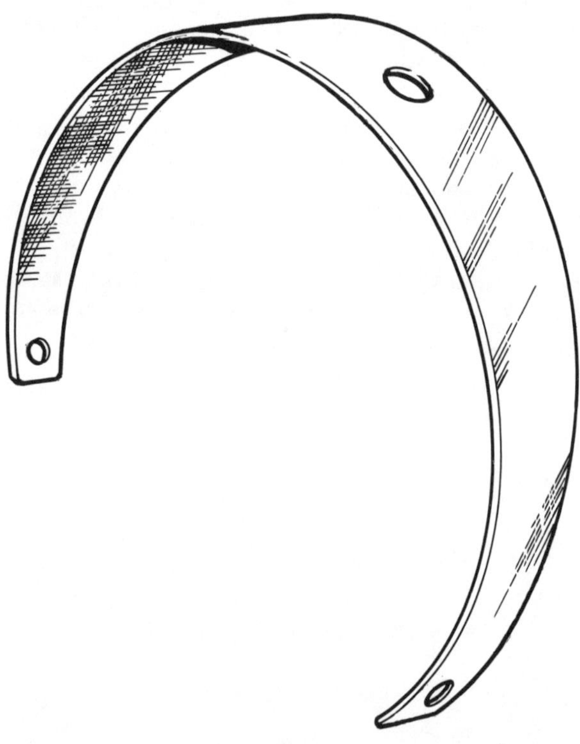

Figure 41. Hour glass clock driving spring.

piece being subsequently veneered. The case was mounted between two turned and tapered wood columns surmounted by turned wood finials, all on a flat wood base. The average height of these clocks was twenty-three inches and the width of the base was about fourteen inches.

The door covered the entire front of the case. At the top was a circular dial glass while the space beneath was fitted with a reverse painted glass tablet that had a small clear space in the center through which to see the bob of the long pendulum.

Inside the clock the paper announced:

Improved
Patent Brass
CLOCKS
manufactured by
JOSEPH IVES
Plainville, Farmington, Ct.

The strike movements were made of wrought brass. Most of them had a duration of thirty hours but a fcw cight-day movements were fitted. A cast iron piece was screwed to the back of the case which was used to support the movement and the spiral wire gong.

A form of inverted wagon spring was used to drive the movement. The spring, illustrated in Fig. 41, was screwed to the roof of the case, and from each end of the string a cord was attached and led to the direct fusees mounted on the winding arbors.

The wheels in the time train and the strike train have seventy-two teeth, and the pinions, which are the fixed lantern type, have six leaves. This ratio enables the great wheel to rotate once in twelve hours and it is to the great wheel of the strike train that the strike count wheel is attached.

Dials are round and made of thin sheet brass, usually with a large hole in the center, and painted with black Roman numerals.

Steeple

In 1844, shortly after he introduced the beehive case, Elias

Ingraham designed the sharp Gothic case, or steeple case as it is now more generally known. Fig. 42 is similar to the original design. The case had straight sides with a gable top and was flanked on either side by a round column surmounted by a tapered spire, the general design being reminiscent of a Gothic arch with steeples. The front carried a single door with two apertures, each containing a piece of glass. The upper half of the door was the dial opening behind which was a white painted dial with black Roman numerals. In the lower portion was a glass tablet which was either reverse painted or acid etched with a surface cut design.

The case met with immediate popularity but Ingraham neglected to safeguard his design with a patent. Inevitably, other makers began producing steeple cases, some with variations of their own.

The majority of cases were veneered with mahogany; others were veneered in walnut or rosewood, and some were further decorated with applied ripple moldings from a variety of impressions.

The usual height was twenty inches, but some were made as small as ten inches while others reached to twenty-four inches.

The columns varied in design and quantity. Some cases were fitted with two columns positioned at the front corners, while others had one at each corner. A few early cases had tapered columns and when surmounted by a finial they resembled ornamented candlesticks.

Early models had a single door but later, when wagon springs were fitted, the base was widened and two doors were fitted, one above the other.

Each maker had his own ideas about the type of movement he wanted to fit, and so it became commonplace that near identical cases were made with widely differing movements.

All movements were brass eight-day or thirty-hour and were spring driven either by coiled spring or wagon spring. They included strap plates, wood and metal fusees, balance wheel and fusee, Silas B. Terry thirty-hour ladder timepiece movements, alarm mechanism, rack and snail strike, count wheel strike, roller pinions, wire gongs and bells.

The first of these clocks were made by the firm Brewster &

Figure 42. Single steeple clock, 8-day brass with count wheel strike. Circa 1844. Clock paper reads:

"Patent Brass Clocks with steel mainspring,
patented and made by Chauncey Jerome,
New Haven, Connecticut."

The glass tablet beneath the dial carries a painting of St. Paul's Cathedral, London.

Figure 43. Double steeple clock, 8-day brass with count wheel strike.Clock paper reads: "Patented Accelerating Lever Spring Eight Day Brass Clock, made and for sale wholesale and retail by Birge and Fuller, Bristol, Conn." Circa 1844 - 1848. The clock was subsequently modified. The wagon spring was removed and in its place was fitted a combination fusee and mainspring assembly incorporated as a separate brass unit secured to the back of the case just below the spiral tape gong.

Ingraham and were fitted with Kirk eight-day and thirty-hour spring driven brass movements with cast iron back plates and wells similar to those movements previously fitted to Ingraham's beehive cases.

The clock paper read:

Patent Spring Eight Day
REPEATING BRASS CLOCKS
MANUFACTURED BY
BREWSTER & INGRAHAMS
Bristol, Conn. U.S.A.

In October 1844 John Birge and Thomas Fuller formed a partnership and the firm of Birge and Fuller almost immediately started producing steeple clocks. At that time Brewster & Ingraham had the monopoly over the use of brass springs and so Birge & Fuller fitted Ives' wagon springs. The bottom portion of the case had to be widened to accommodate the leaf spring and the height had to be increased to make room for the winding arrangement.

The upper portion carried a single door with a glass tablet below the dial opening, and the lower and wider part of the case was fitted with its own door and glass tablet. To distinguish the case from the original design it is frequently referred to as the steeple-on-frame case.

Birge & Fuller made two models, an eight-day and a thirty-hour. The eight-day was fitted with two candlestick type steeples on each side of the case, and was about twenty-four inches high. The movement included a count wheel strike and had roller pinions to both wheel trains. Stamped on the front plate was:

Birge & Fuller
Bristol, Conn. U.S.A.

Figure 44. Double steeple clock, 8-day brass with count wheel strike. Made by Birge and Fuller. Circa 1844 - 1848.

On the clock paper were the words:

J. IVES PATENT
ACCELERATING LEVER SPRING
EIGHT DAY BRASS CLOCKS
made and for sale Wholesale and Retail by
BIRGE & FULLER
BRISTOL, CONN.

The thirty hour clock had only one column at each side and was approximately twenty-one inches high.

Another variant is illustrated in Figs. 43, 44 and 45. This design is known as double steeple or steeple-on-steeple and was fitted with eight-day or thirty-hour movements, not all of which were driven by wagon springs. In 1847 steel coil springs became more generally available and Birge & Fuller discontinued fitting wagon springs in favor of coil springs with fusees, but they retained the steeple-on-steeple case design. The firm of Brewster & Ingraham continued with the original design as did the majority of other makers.

Acorn

A unique design in clock cases was introduced in 1845 by Jonathan Clark Brown of Forestville Manufacturing Co. Because of its shape, it became known as the acorn clock. The framework, door and side arms were carefully molded from laminated wood and mounted on a laminated wood base. The upper portion of the door carried the dial glass and below was a reverse painted glass tablet, frequently of State buildings. The cases were graceful and beautifully finished and were usually a little more than two feet high.

The white circular dial with its black Roman numerals took up a central position in the acorn-shaped top. The surrounding areas on the door glass were decorated with colorful emblems or floral designs. The dials were sometimes marked Forestville Manufacturing Co.

Inside the earliest cases the labels read:

EIGHT DAY
SPRING CLOCKS
Manufactured by
J.C. BROWN
BRISTOL, CONN.

Those that were made shortly after carried labels with the words:

Patent applied for Sept. 1848
EIGHT DAY BRASS CLOCKS
Springs with equalized power, warranted not to fail;
Manufactured and sold by
FORESTVILLE MANUFACTURING COMPANY
J.C. Brown Bristol Conn.

The movement was an eight-day brass with skeleton plates, a count wheel strike and an anchor escapement. Stamped on the bottom of the front plate was:

J.C.BROWN of Forestville Mfg. Co.

The first of these clocks had wood reverse fusees with coil springs that were housed in recesses cut in a block of wood secured to the back of the case at the bottom. Subsequent clocks had the spring fusee units, with spring barrels, mounted in metal frames screwed to the back of the case. In both arrangements, the gut line was led from the fusee direct to the winding drum in the movement.

In 1848 J.C. Brown began to simplify the design of the case, presumably to reduce the cost of manufacture, but in so doing he destroyed the graceful appearance of the original design and replaced it with a case that was less attractive.

Frames, doors, side arms and bases were no longer laminated. In many instances, side arms were omitted altogether. Bases were made from low cost timber and veneered. The lower protion of the case was no longer rounded, the sides were made vertical and were squared to a flat bottom. The height of these later cases was increased to anything up to three feet.

Inside the case the movement remained the same but the spring fusee unit was raised from the bottom of the case and attached to the bottom of the movement. A few late production clocks were

Figure 45. Double steeple clock. Circa 1844. Clock paper reads: "Improved Steel Spring Eight Day Brass Clock, made and for sale wholesale and retail by John Birge, Bristol, Conn." The motive power is the same as Fig. 43, except that the fusees are wood and the housing of fusee and mainspring are of wood.

Figure 46. Acorn clock. Forestville Manufacturing Co., Bristol, Conn. Circa 1845 - 1850. 8-day brass with count wheel strike. Powered by a combination mainspring and fusee unit secured to the bottom of the case. Door tablet shows The Merchants Exchange, Philadelphia.

Figure 46A. Inside the case of Fig. 46.

driven directly by coiled springs without the aid of fusees.

Lever or Marine

Weight driven clocks with pendulums were far from being portable. They were heavy and difficult to carry, and they had to be level to allow the pendulum to swing with a regular beat.

When coil springs were introduced as motive power the reduction in the weight of the clock as a result of eliminating the suspending weights was considerable, and cases could be made much smaller. The pendulum however still remained, and to transport the clock the pendulum had to be held from swinging, the clock had to be leveled in its new position and the hands reset if any appreciable loss of time had taken place.

About 1848 William Barnbridge Barnes of Bristol developed a spring driven thirty-hour brass movement that was controlled by a spring balance wheel. Any clock fitted with such an escapement could be moved continuously without interference to the function of the movement and without any loss or gain. The design for complete portability had been accomplished.

In 1849 Barnes entered into partnership with Ebenezer Hendrick and the firm of Hendrick, Barnes & Co. produced balance wheel movements for sale to other firms who cased and sold them. These clocks became known as lever or marine clocks. Barnes did not cover his balance wheel idea with a patent and it was not long before other makers were actively engaged in producing lever movements.

In addition to the fitting of lever movements to currect case designs of wall and shelf clocks, this new concept of clock movement control provided case designers with the opportunity of producing a new range of designs that could not have been used with pendulums. There began to appear on the market an endless variety of small clocks for export and for sale in America. Among the most popular were wood cases veneered in walnut, mahogany or rosewood, and papier-mache cases that were Japanned and decorated with mother-of-pearl inlay and sea shells. These clocks were the forerunners of the better known low priced round metal-cased alarm clocks with a bell on the top or at the back. By 1880 they were being produced in large quantities, and after the turn of the century the export of these small alarm clocks had become big business.

Calendar

The majority of tall case clocks were fitted with some kind of calendar mechanism, either simple or perpetual, but when these clocks went out of fashion in favor of wood shelf clocks, perpetual calendar mechanism was discontinued. Some shelf clocks and wall clocks were fitted with simple calendar work, *i.e.* a hand and days of the month marked outside the minute ring on the dial, but it was not until about 1854 that perpetual calendar work put in a reappearance. Clocks so fitted soon became popular and remained so until the early years of the twentieth century.

The first American patent to be issued for a calendar mechanism was granted to John H.H. Hawes, Ithaca, N.Y. in 1853. The design did not include automatic correction for leap years and was therefore never used. Subsequent patents were issued to: William H. Atkins and Joseph C. Burritt, 1854; James E. Mix and Eugene M. Mix, 1860; Benjamin Bennett Lewis, 1862; Henry B. Horton, 1865; Randall T. Andrews, 1876; Daniel Jackson Gale, 1877.

The design produced by Atkins and Burritt was further developed by the Mix Brothers and then used by Seth Thomas Clock Co. in their calendar clocks from 1862 until 1876.

Randall T. Andrews was an employee of Seth Thomas Clock Co., and when he developed a calendar mechanism in 1876 his employer used the design in preference to that of Atkins and Burritt.

The calendar mechanism developed by Benjamin Bennett Lewis was used by a number of clockmakers, the most prominent being E. Graham Co., Welch, Spring & Co., E.N. Welch Manufacturing Co., and Burwell & Carter.

After Henry B. Horton was granted a patent for his calendar mechanism he commercialized his idea by forming Ithaca Calendar Clock Co.

In 1875 Southern Calendar Clock Co. was formed. They were essentially a selling organization and their calendar clocks were made by Seth Thomas Co. under the trademark, Fashion.

Daniel Jackson Gale developed a complicated mechanism and dial arrangement which was fitted to calendar clocks made by E.N. Welch Manufacturing Co.

Most of the large clock companies made calendar clocks, and between them they produced a wide variety of styles. Probably the two companies with the greatest sales were Southern Calendar Clock Co. and Ithaca Calendar Clock Co., both of which specialized in calendar clocks and sold nothing else.

The majority of cases were made of walnut, but rosewood veneer was quite usual. The most popular arrangement was to have two dials, one above the other, and as a consequence the cases were taller than they were wide. They varied in height from about eighteen inches to about four feet for shelf clocks and about five feet for wall clocks.

Generally the upper dial was devoted to time and the lower dial to calendar information, but there were variations. The more usual arrangements were:

Single Dial

(a) Time with extra hand pointing to the day of the month marked outside the minute ring.

(b) Time plus day of the week outside the minute ring and day of the month outside again. The days of the week were painted continuously around a disc and were displayed through a series of windows coincident with the day of the month markings. In this way, every date had a corresponding day of the week that changed automatically at the beginning of a new month by rotating the disc. Above the dial a small window in the case displayed the month of the year.

(c) Typical of the Gale patent, the day of the month was marked around the edge of the dial. Inside were four subsidiary dials. The upper dial indicated time; on the left was day of the week, on the right was phase of the moon, and the lower dial indicated month of the year together with times of sunrise and sunset.

Two Dials

UPPER DIAL	LOWER DIAL
Time only, with or without seconds hand.	Day of the month marked around the edge and a center hand.
Time plus an extra hand pointing to day of the week marked outside minute ring.	Two hands rotating at the center. One hand for the day of the month marked around the edge, and the other hand for an inner ring of month of the year markings.
Time only, with or without seconds hand.	Day of the month marked around the edge. Day of the week painted on a horizontal roller that appeared through a slot at the left of the dial. Similarly the month of the year appeared on the right.

All movements were made of brass and, with the exception of a few wall clocks that ran for thirty days, had a running time of eight days. The majority of movements were spring driven but weights were sometimes used in both shelf and wall clocks. Almost all movements had strike mechanisms and very occasionally a movement was fitted with alarm.

The calendar mechanism of a two dial clock was separately mounted beneath the movement and was invariably operated by vertical rods actuated by a cam driven by the wheel train of the clock movement.

The following are extracts from typical clock papers of clocks with two dials:

1. Spring driven calendar clock by Ithaca Calendar Clock Co., Ithaca, N.Y.

The time now stands at 5 minutes before 11 p.m.

If the clock is to be set in the morning, turn the minute hand forward until the right hour is reached.

If the clock is to be set in the afternoon, turn the minute hand forward through twelve hours and then to the right hour.

The calendar changes at midnight.

Never move the hour hand by itself, as the calendar would not change at the proper hour.

To set the calendar, raise the wire at the top of the clock and turn the calendar hand forward (never) backward) until the right month and day of month is shown.

Still holding up the wire turn the day of the week upward till right.

Caution - Use no oil in the calendar. It is not needed and will work only injury when used by attracting dust and clogging the machine.

Every clock before leaving the works is tested thoroughly, both as to time and calendar, and the calendar being set on the right year when the clock is packed, will give the leap year and other Februarys correctly unless interfered with, or worked ahead of time. But if this should occur, it can readily be set right as follows. Raise the wire as above, turn the pointer forward until a February is shown, and then place the pointer on the figure 29, drop the wire and if the point cannot be moved you have a leap year February. If the pointer is not held fast on the figure 29, continue the process until it is. Calling this the last leap year, work forward as before to the right year and month.

2. Weight driven calendar clock by Seth Thomas Clock Co., Thomaston, Conn.

Make the clock stand firmly in the desired position. See that the cords are on the pulleys. Hang on the weights, and set the clock running.

Remove the screw confining the month roll. If the calendar does not show right, take hold of the rod at the left; and pump or work it up and down until the proper day of the week appears.

Work the rod at the right in the same manner until the right month appears; then continue to work the rod until the correct day of the month is indicated by the band. The clock now shows 5 o'clock in the morning; turn it by the minute hand to the right time of day.

Keep the clock wound up. Should it run down, and in consequence the calendar get behind a day or two, turn it by the minute hand until the calendar shows right. This calendar is perpetual and, if it is correctly set up will not fail to show the proper day of the week, the month, and the day of the month, including the 29th day of February in leap year.

Timby Solar Globe Timepiece

In 1863 Theodore R. Timby was granted a patent covering what he called his solar timepiece, Fig. 47. The cases were made of oak or walnut. Mounted in the center was a terrestrial globe that rotated on a horizontal axis and which was driven by an eight-day brass movement. Attached to the circumference of the globe was a flat graduated ring which rotated with the globe once in every twenty-four hours. The ring was graduated in twenty-four equal divisions to represent the hours, the spaces being numbered 1 to 12 twice. Each division was sub-divided into sixty equal divisions to represent minutes. Below the globe was another dial that rotated once a minute and which was divided into sixty equal divisions to represent seconds. The time was read from the dials by referring to a pointer or index attached to the case.

These timepieces were made by Lewis E. Whiting at Saratoga Springs and then shipped to Gilman Joslin in Boston for him to fit his patent globe of the earth.

Timby's patent included the provision of an adjustment between the hour ring and the globe, and Timby claimed that this adjustment made it possible to read solar time as well as mean time, and to note the difference in time between any two locations. Unfortunately, many of the design details mentioned in the patent specification were omitted by the manufacturer, resulting in the globe being little more than a novelty.

About six hundred timepieces were made, all of which were numbered, but they proved to be unpopular and manufacture ceased in 1870.

Walnut and Oak

During the latter part of the nineteenth century some of the bigger clock companies manufactured clocks with cases of walnut and of oak. The majority of cases included a large expanse, the biggest part of which was above the dial. Much effort was expended in providing them with an excess of decorative detail that was a little overpowering and sometimes rather grotesque. Even so, they were robust, reliable, reasonably priced and they sold well.

WALNUT CLOCKS (1865 - 1900). Cases were made in natural or black walnut and their heights ranged from nineteen inches to about twenty-six inches. The lower portion of the glass paneled door was decorated with foliage, birds or geometric designs produced by stencil or etching.

The designs of the tops of the cases suggested architectural features such as balconies, coping-stones and rooftops, many of which had an eastern appearance.

Carved, turned and fluted side columns were used, sometimes surmounted by finials. Most cases were embellished with shallow carving, and applied carved figure heads and motifs were not unusual.

The movements were eight-day or thirty-hour brass with strike. Frequently an alarm mechanism was fitted. The round white dials were approximately five inches in diameter with black Roman

Figure 47. Oak Timby solar timepiece.

numerals. Pendulums were made of brass and usually very decorative.

OAK CLOCKS (1875 - 1910). The cases of these clocks were made of impressed and stained oak, and in general construction they were similar to the walnut clocks. A movement case with a glass paneled door in a wood frame was mounted on a base. The shape of the door top was either three-sided, four-sided or flat. Around the movement case on both sides and across the top was a large flat area of any shape that increased the height of the clock to about twenty-four inches. This area was decorated with bold and varied designs produced by a metal press applied to the wood after the wood had been made pliable by immersing in steam. The effect caused the designs to stand out in relief rather like that of embossed work.

A popular theme was to produce a circular plaque at the top in which to portray the head of a famous American politician or military commander. Elsewhere on the area the subject of the design was appropriate to the figurehead. The supporting design for an army general might well include regimental flags, cannons and cannon balls, bugles and swords. For a navy admiral it was usual to include a ship under his command with supporting designs embodying anchors, stars and flags. Past presidents of the United States were a favorite as were important and well known public buildings. Other subjects for decoration were floral and foliage interlaced with intricate designs.

The lower portion of the door glass below the dial was either etched or stenciled with similar motifs and designs but rarely enough to prevent the motion of the pendulum being visible.

The edge of the base was usually finished with a molding which was sometimes impressed with an appropriate design.

The movements were eight-day brass, spring driven without fusee, usually with a half-hour strike, and sometimes with an alarm mechanism. The round brass pendulum bobs were mounted in an ornate brass frame producing a very decorative pendulum.

The round dials were white with black Roman numerals, and

Figure 48. Walnut shelf clock. Circa 1880. Ansonia Clock Co. 8-day strike.

Figure 49. Walnut shelf clock. Circa 1880. Ansonia Clock Co. 8-day strike. Model "KING".

Figure 50. Walnut shelf clock. Circa 1890. Ansonia Clock Co. 8-day strike and alarm.

the two winding holes were usually at IV and VIII. A few of these clocks had calendar dials. The days of the month were painted outside the minute track and the movement was fitted with a slender, centrally mounted hand which carried the crescent of a new moon on its inner end.

Black Mantel

About 1875 black mantel clocks appeared. They enjoyed a popularity that continued until the early years of the twentieth century. Most large manufacturing companies produced them but possibly more were made by the Ansonia Clock Co. than any other firm.

The cases were made of black marble, black cast iron or black enameled wood that gave the appearance of ebony. Size varied from nine and one-half inches to eighteen inches long, and ten inches to twelve and one-half inches high. Usually they had flat tops. The base was invariably flat but sometimes black or gilded cast feet were fitted.

An applied ornament was frequently added to each side often taking the form of a lion's head or drop handle. Long cases were adorned with round, reeded or flat columns surmounted by capitals sometimes presenting an appearance not unlike that of ancient Greek temples.

Dials were usually white and round measuring from five inches to seven inches in diameter. The numerals were black Arabic or Roman. Some black dials were used with gilt Arabic numerals and hands. Dials were protected by glass mounted in a hinged gilt decorative bezel.

The movements were spring-driven, pendulum-controlled, brass, eight-day with strike and sometimes alarm. The strike was rack and snail that functioned at the half hour as well as the hour. Spiral gongs were used but a few clocks were fitted with a bell for the half hour.

Many of these clocks were provided with the novelty of having the movement escapement fitted in front of the dial beneath the twelve o'clock position. It was also a visual indication that the movement was functioning.

CHAPTER 4

Wall Clocks

Wag-on-Wall

THE COST OF making a tall case clock and fitting an eight-day brass strike movement was high and only a few families in each community were able to afford such a luxury. Nevertheless, cvcry houschold needed to know the time and there was, therefore, a big demand for a low-priced clock.

This resulted in the introduction of thirty-hour wood strike movements. The wheels and frame plates were made of oak but the escape wheel continued to be made of brass, and pivots and pinions of steel. The movements were supplied with dials, hands and weights and were known as hang-up or wag-on-wall clocks. The tall cases were purchased later, if required.

Banjo

About 1800 Simon Willard began developing a new design of wall case and in 1802 he was granted a patent for what he called his Patent Timepiece. The movement was small and simple, there being no strike mechanism, and it was a good timekeeper. The case was symmetrical and well proportioned. Many were exquisitely painted in bright colors and the effect was that of graceful ornamentation. The shape earned for itself the name banjo. The success of these timepieces was instantaneous and their popularity continued throughout the first half of the century.

Figure 51. Oak wag-on-wall clock by R. Whiting, Conn. Circa 1810 - 1820. 30-hour wood movement with count wheel strike. Painted dial with colored floral and gold designs in spandrels and break-arch. Subsidiary dials indicate seconds and days of the month.

Figure 52. Wag-on-wall clock with painted dial 13½ inches diameter. Circa 1820.

Figure 53. Banjo timepiece. Probably by Willard. Circa 1805 - 1806. The lower tablet is painted S. Willard's Patent. On the reverse side of both tablets are the words Willard & Nolen, Boston.

Simon Willard's banjo timepieces can generally be divided into three categories:

1. The very early models
2. The standard models
3. The presentation models which were usually the most decorative and expensive and which were only made to special order.

The very early cases were plain. They were made of mahogany, with the back sometimes of pine, and were decorated with fine inlay work. The bezel for the dial glass was made of brass as were the ornamental side pieces, but there were no painted front glasses or decorative base bracket. It is doubtful whether many of these timepieces have survived.

The timepieces that followed those early models were more elaborately decorated and have come to be regarded as Simon Willard's standard model. Mahogany continued to be the chosen wood for the case but the front was fitted with painted glass tablets in a variety of bright colors. The cases were made by different casemakers but always to Simon Willard's design.

Mounted on top of the case was a finial, usually an acorn, made of brass or gilded turned wood. It is thought by many students of Simon Willard's banjo timepieces that he never used a spread eagle to adorn the top of his cases and any that do exist are subsequent replacements.

The top of the case at the rear was cut away just below the finial to receive a flush fitting brass hanger plate. These plates on early models were held to the case by one screw, but on later models the size of the plate was increased and two fixing screws were used.

The round dial glass bezel was hinged on the right and held shut by a screw catch at the left. The glass was flat and held to the bezel from the inside by small brackets screwed to the bezel. The very early models had two brackets and subsequent models had three.

Dials were made of thick flat sheet iron painted with many coats of white enamel and then painted with black Roman numerals and a minute ring. The winding hole was adjacent to the two o'clock position. The dial was secured to the case by slotted screws that had a right-angled arm at the head. When the screw was turned the arm at the head swung in front of the dial and held it in place. The hands were distinctive, always very slender with extremely fine barbs filed at the ends.

From beneath the dial the neck of the case tapered slightly outward and downward, flanked by ornamental brass side pieces, and mounted on a rectangular base fitted with a full size door.

Secured to the front face of the neck, and mounted in the framework of the door, were hand painted glass tablets held in position by short lengths of triangular section wood that were glued and pinned. The tablets were surrounded by narrow cross-banded veneer of mahogany, rosewood or curled maple.

Simon Willard employed an English artist to paint the tablets. The name and background of this man is not known but his work most certainly is. The brushwork was fine and delicate, and the colors woven into the designs were the work of a very capable artist. This Englishman had an apprentice, Charles Bullard, who took over the work about 1848. It is the opinion of some collectors that the quality of Bullard's work does not match up to that of his master but, be that as it may, all known examples hold pride of place in any collection.

The slender brass side pieces were carefully filed to shape and each was held to the mahogany case by pins. Three holes were drilled in the side pieces, one at the top, one at the bottom and one in the center. The pins were inserted into these holes and tapped into the wood.

The door in the base was to provide access to the pendulum bob if the movement needed to be regulated, and to secure the pendulum from swinging when moving the timepiece. The pendulum was held by a brass slide that engaged the lower end of the pendulum rod.

The door was held in the closed position by a square-ended screw that had a right-angled arm at its inner end. To unlock the door the winding key was placed over the exposed square end and turned. As the screw rotated, so the arm at the inner end moved away from behind the framework of the case, leaving the door free to swing open.

Painted on the door tablet were the words S. WILLARD PATENT or S. WILLARD'S PATENT.

Figure 54. Banjo timepiece. There is no signature to indicate the maker, nor are there any markings to suggest place of origin. 8-day brass movement. Circa 1805 - 1825.

The movements were brass, eight-day with heavy plates and wheels, all finely finished. Two long, blued steel slotted screws were used to hold the movement to the case back. These screws passed through both plates of the movement but the rear end of the screws was reduced in diameter and passed through a reduced hole in the back plate. This arrangement insured that the rear plate was held firmly against the case back by the shoulder on the screw without pulling on the front plate.

The pendulum was hung in front of the front plate, thereby placing the regulation nut in a more accessible position. The pendulum rod was made of iron, and close to its upper end it was shaped to form a horizontal rectangle to clear the projecting center pinion. The pendulum bob was made of lead and covered in thin brass sheet.

Simon Willard's presentation timepieces were made to order, frequently for special occasions, and were more costly than his standard model. The basic design remained unchanged, the cases continued to be made of mahogany and the same movements were fitted; it was in the quality of the decoration that the difference lay.

The cases were white enameled and gilded. Finials sometimes took the form of eagles. The white enameled dials were decorated with brightly colored flowers, and the brass bezel, together with the brass side pieces, were highly polished. Only on presentation timepieces did Simon Willard allow his name, S. WILLARD PATENT, to be painted on the dials.

The bright colored, hand painted glass tablet on the neck included a cross-hatch design that resembled the finest lace. It was frequently applied in gold leaf.

By way of contrast to the standard model, the door tablets were painted with landscapes, ships, naval encounters or anything else the customer preferred. Beneath the base was attached a gilded ornamental bracket. Frequently the neck and the door were edged with a gilded rope-like trim or gilt beading.

Simon Willard did not use clock papers.

It was not long before Simon's younger brother Aaron began making banjo timepieces, but he was less conservative in his ideas than his brother.

Figure 55. Banjo timepiece. Circa 1810 - 1820. An unusual design. Mahogany. At the bottom of the lower tablet is the name Jabez Baldwin.

Simon confined his most colorful and decorative cases to his presentation models whereas Aaron produced similar cases on a more regular basis. It was not unusual for him to fit movements with strike mechanisms, and when this was done the width of the neck was increased to accommodate the additional hanging weight.

Aaron had his name painted on the neck tablet and his signature appeared on the dial.

About 1823 Aaron Willard retired and his son Aaron Willard, Jr. took over the business. An example of his clock paper is shown below:

DIRECTIONS FOR PUTTING UP THE TIMEPIECE

Drive a brad in the wall where it is to be placed and suspend the TIMEPIECE upon it. Open the lower door which is unfastened by turning the button a little forward with the key. Loosen the pendulum by which the TIMEPIECE may be plumbed, observing that it hangs free of the case and in a line with the point where it was confined, then screw it to the wall with two screws thro' the back. Put the pendulum in motion. The weight is already wound up. Set it with the minute hand which may be moved backwards or forwards. To make the TIMEPIECE go faster raise the pendulum ball by the screw at the bottom, to make it go slower, lower the ball with the same screw.

These TIMEPIECES are an improvement upon all others, as they go by a weight instead of a spring, and the pendulum being of a longer calculation than in any other small pieces renders it more accurate and has proved to keep better time. The President of the United States having granted a Patent for them, they are made by licence from the Patentee by Aaron Willard Junr. Washington St. Boston, near Roxbury, MASSACHUSETTS.

The popularity of these timepieces became so widespread that, despite the existence of a patent, other clockmakers were unable to resist the temptation to copy, and so large numbers of banjos

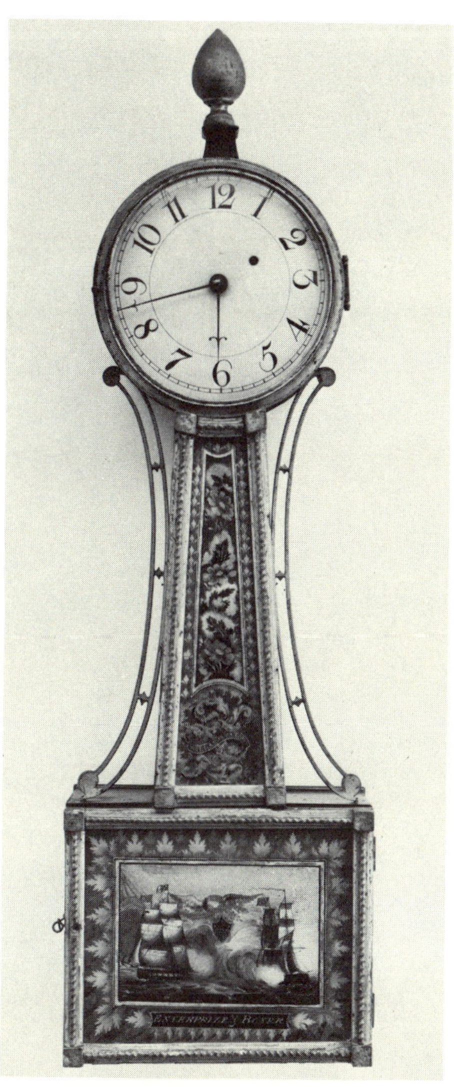

Figure 56. Banjo timepiece. Circa 1813 - 1815. The words Willard's Patent in scroll at base of neck. The bottom tablet carries a painted picture of a naval encounter and bears the caption : Enterprize & Boxer.

Figure 57. Banjo timepiece. The words Willard's Patent appear in scroll at base of neck. Circa 1815. The picture in the bottom tablet shows a naval battle. The caption reads Constitution & Cuerriere. Height including bracket is 33½ inches.

Figure 58. Banjo timepiece. Made by Nathaniel Monroe, Baltimore. Circa 1815. Signature in scroll at base of neck. Thermometer attached to front of upper tablet. Lower painted tablet has oval of clear glass to observe pendulum bob. Height including bracket 39 inches.

Figure 59. Lyre timepiece. Possibly by Elnathan Taber. Circa 1835 - 1840. Scratched on iron plate behind dial are the words Cleaned by E. Taber March 16 1847. Taber was apprenticed to the Willards and made clocks for Simon and Aaron. Height including bracket 40 inches.

began to appear, most with slight variations to Simon Willard's Patent Timepiece.

The height of banjo cases varied from about thirty inches to about forty five inches, but between 1840 and 1850 it was not unusual for them to appear in railroad stations and measuring up to seven feet in height.

Lyre

The neck of the lyre was shaped in the fashion of the musical instrument of that name and was usually framed in carved foliage or scroll work. The head was the same as that of a banjo timepiece and from beneath the head a set of ornamental strings was frequently fitted which extended downward to the base of the neck to complete the illusion of a string instrument. Sometimes the front panel of the neck was delicately painted with floral designs in bright colors. Some cases did not have a rectangular base with a painted glass tablet in the door; the molded or carved bracket was attached direct to the base of the neck. Cases were usually made of mahogany and their height varied from about thirty-eight inches to about forty-four inches.

The movements were brass eight-day weight driven. Occasionally they were fitted with strike mechanisms and less frequently alarm mechanisms were fitted.

The origin of these timepieces is unknown and there are many examples that are not marked with the name of the maker. It is known that they were being made in 1810 and continued until at least 1840.

Girandole

The girandole has many times been referred to as America's most beautiful clock. It was developed by Lemuel Curtis about 1814 and became so called because of its similarity in appearance to that of a girandole looking glass with its gem studded pendant.

Curtis made about fifty of these timepieces between 1814 and 1818 and they are, therefore, extremely rare.

The cases were made either of veneered mahogany with the front finished in gold leaf, or the entire case was gold-leafed. The paintings on the glass tablets are superb, particularly those on the convex glass of the pendant door. The average height of a girandole is about forty-four inches.

Dials were white enamel with black Arabic numerals and were signed L. CURTIS PATENT. The words CURTIS PATENT also appeared on the glass tablet of the neck.

Movements were brass, eight-day, weight driven.

Joseph Ives' Looking Glass

In 1817 Joseph Ives introduced a large, eight-day, weight-driven brass movement with roller pinions and fitted it into a wall case that carried a full length mirror in the door. He applied for a patent in 1817, but it was not until 1822 before it was finally granted.

Considerable care and time were taken in the making of these movements, resulting in high cost of production. For this reason they were not a commercial proposition, and after three years no more were made.

The first cases were in the form of rectangular picture frames, made with a deep molding of gilded gesso and wood beading. They measured approximately twenty inches wide and forty inches high.

The movement had solid plates made from cast and hammered brass that was fitted with bronze and ivory bushes. The bronze bushes were inserted from the outside to a depth of half the thickness of the plate; these were to support the arbor pivots. The ivory bushes were pressed in from the inside to reduce wear from lateral movement of the arbors.

The wheels were machined from brass castings and were fitted with roller pinions. Strike was by rack and snail mechanism, and the short pendulum had a half second beat.

This style of clock is rare because only a limited number was made.

Ives then changed the style of case and fitted movements with long pendulums with a one second rating. The tops of these cases were decorated with scrolls and finials like those of Eli Terry's pillar and scroll clocks.

The doors were made to the full width of the case and reached

Figure 60. Girandole by Lemuel Curtis, Concord, Mass. Circa 1816. Signature on dial L. Curtis Patent. The reverse painting in the lower tablet shows a biblical scene from the book of Kings. The caption reads Elisha Restores The Schunammites Son. Height 46 inches.

Figure 61. Jewelers regulator believed to be by John Sawin. Circa 1850. Sawin was apprenticed to Aaron Willard, Jr. Walnut case decorated with Victorian style wood carving. 8-day brass weight driven movement with dead beat escapement, Harrison's maintaining spring, and a one-second Gridiron compensating pendulum. Dial fitted with sweep seconds hand. Overall height 82 inches.

Figure 62. Long drop regulator by Jerome & Co. Circa 1880. 8-day time only. Walnut case.

to the base of the scroll top. The full height of the case was approximately five feet with a width of about twenty inches.

The most usual decoration was a three inch wide reeded molding surmounted by a curved bracket resembling cyma molding placed on each side of the mirror, and which extended to the full height of the door.

Below the mirror was a reverse painted glass tablet with a clear oval of glass through which the bob of the pendulum could be seen.

The first of these long pendulum movements had open front plates, but in 1820 Joseph Ives began making similar eight-day movements with solid iron plates with bronze bushes, and with a roller verge escapement.

The arrangement for weights and lines in all these clocks was as illustrated in Fig. 64(b).

Cases similar to Joseph Ives' looking glass clock were made by other makers up to about 1835, but not in any quantity.

Regulator

The name was originally intended for timepieces with precision eight-day, weight-driven, long pendulum movements capable of accurate timekeeping. They were fitted in wall cases and include such refinements as temperature compensating pendulums, maintaining power and frequently deadbeat escapements. They were made as early as 1840, but it was not until about 1870 that they were produced in large quantities.

CHAPTER 5
Movements and Mechanisms

Wheel Train

A SERIES OF gear wheels and pinions in mesh is known as a train of wheels. All clocks, timepieces and watches have wheel trains which are used to transmit the motive power of falling weights or coiled springs under tension. In the case of a time train the motive power is transmitted to the escapement and so to the pendulum or balance. The strike and the chime of a clock have their own wheel trains.

It is the time train that drives the hands, and we know that the individual wheels that drive the hands must rotate clockwise viewed from the front and that their respective speeds have to be one revolution per twelve hours for the hour hand, one revolution per hour for the minute hand, and if a seconds hand is fitted, it must rotate one revolution per minute.

With these facts in mind the clock or watchmakers must decide how many wheels will be required, what must be the gear ratio between each pair of wheels, the direction of rotation of each wheel, how long the pendulum or balance spring must be, and details of layout. Wheel trains vary but once the basic principle of a simple movement is understood, it is not difficult to follow a more complex movement.

When a seconds hand is fitted it is always driven by the escape wheel, but if the maker does not intend to include a seconds hand, then the speed of rotation of the escape wheel is not confined to one revolution per minute nor is the direction of rotation necessarily clockwise, viewed from the front.

The minute and hour hands are driven by their own set of wheels and pinions known collectively as the motion train which derives its motive power from the time train.

TIME TRAIN

Consider the time train in Fig. 68, which is part of the movement shown in Fig. 79. This movement is fitted with a seconds hand mounted on the escape wheel arbor and is regulated by a pendulum which must have a beat of one second.

We know that an anchor escapement will release the teeth of an escape wheel in order to allow the wheel to rotate half the distance between a pair of teeth with each swing of the pendulum. This means that the equivalent of a half tooth is released in one second and therefore in sixty seconds a total of thirty teeth will be released. If the escape wheel is cut with thirty teeth, then the wheel will make one revolution in one minute which is the requirement for a seconds hand.

The escape pinion has six leaves and the third wheel has thirty teeth; the gear ratio is therefore 5:1, *i.e.*the third wheel rotates one fifth the speed of the escape wheel. If we follow these calculations back to the great wheel we find the ratio between the third pinion and the second wheel is 6:1 and the ratio between the second pinion and the great wheel is 4:1, all of which means that the ratio between the great wheel and the escape wheel is 5x6x4 = 120:1. The speed of the great wheel must therefore be:

1/120 rev./min. = 1 rev./120 mins or ½ rev./hour

MOTION TRAIN

This is sometimes referred to as the motion work or dial wheels. From Figs. 68 and 80 it will be seen that the minute wheel with thirty-six teeth is driven by the great wheel arbor and must therefore travel at the same speed, *i.e.* half a revolution per hour. The center wheel or minute pinion with eighteen teeth will therefore rotate one revolution per hour, which is twice as fast, and it is on the center wheel or minute pinion pipe that the minute hand is carried.

The hour pinion with eight leaves also rotates at one half revolution per hour, but because the hour wheel has forty-eight teeth it must rotate one revolution per twelve hours as required by the hour hand. The number of teeth and leaves given to the wheels and pinions must provide a ratio of 12:1. In this instance we have 36/8 x 48/18 = 12.

This simple movement illustrates how a pendulum with a known rating, together with a train of wheels with predetermined gear ratios, can provide drives for the hands at the correct speeds and direction of rotation.

Verge and Crown Wheel Escapement

This is the original form of escapement and was first used in the earliest medieval clocks during the thirteenth century. It consists of a cylindrical wheel with triangular-shaped teeth, creating the impression of a crown, and a steel verge carrying two pallets spaced at a distance equal to the diameter of the crown wheel and forming an angle a little over one hundred degrees.

The verge is mounted centrally across the mouth of the crown wheel, and at one end is attached the pendulum crutch. The motive power tries to drive the train of gears but the verge escapement holds the train in check. When a crown wheel tooth meets a pallet, the tooth pushes the pallet forward and clear, and the tooth escapes. At this point the tooth diametrically opposite encounters the other pallet and the sequence of movement is repeated.

In Fig. 63, tooth C is pushing against pallet A causing the verge to turn counter-clockwise giving impetus to the pendulum. When tooth C escapes, the crown wheel continues to rotate until tooth D is halted by pallet B, but the verge and pendulum still retain some of their mass balance impetus, and it pushes against tooth D causing the crown wheel to recoil.

The motive power then takes over and tooth D pushes against pallet B, causing the verge to turn clockwise, giving impetus to the pendulum in the opposite direction. When tooth D escapes from pallet B the cycle of movement is repeated, and each time a tooth escapes, the crown wheel turns and then recoils. Meanwhile, the

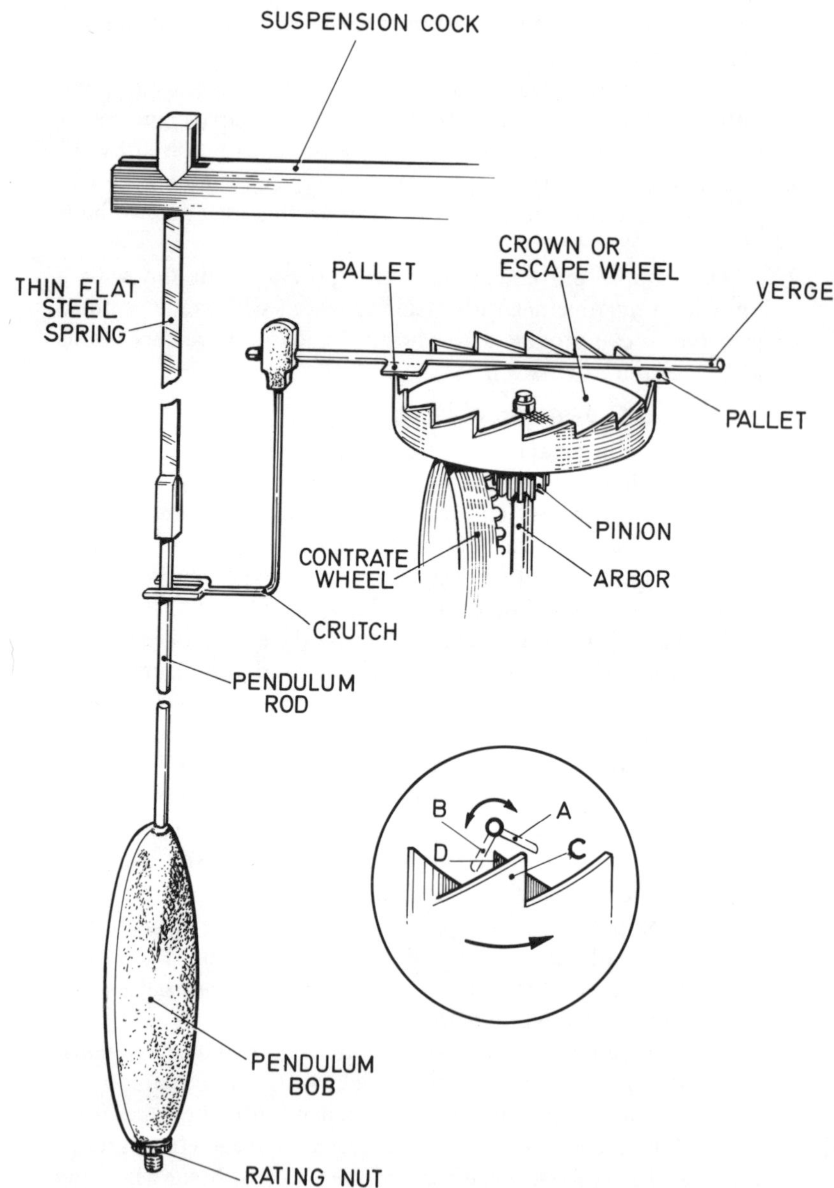

Figure 63. Verge and Crown Wheel Escapement.

pendulum continues to swing first in one direction and then in the other.

Lines and Weights

KEY WINDING (Fig. 64). The most simple arrangement is shown at (a). Here the weight hangs directly from the drum and the movement will function so long as the weight continues to fall. The length of the line, therefore, controls how long the movement will function before rewinding is necessary.

The arrangement at (b) introduces a pulley which is frequently secured at the top of the case. This has the effect of increasing the distance the weight has to travel to reach the floor, and therefore the running time of the movement is increased.

A further improvement is obtained by using the arrangement as at (c). The free end of the line is attached to the top of the case and a pulley is fastened to the weight. The rate of fall of the weight is halved; in other words the weight takes twice as long to reach the bottom, but twice as much line is required. Unlike arrangements (a) and (b) that had only one point of suspension for the weight, arrangement (c) has two suspension points, *i.e.* the top of the case and the drum. This means that the pull of the weight is shared equally by these two points, and now only half is available to drive the movement. To overcome this the weight must be doubled.

In the last arrangement (d) a pulley has been added. This further increases the length of the line and thereby increases the running time of the movement at one winding.

PULL-UP WINDING (Fig. 79). Two weights of differing poundage are suspended by lines wound around the drum in opposite directions. Sometimes a continuous line was used, the center of which was attached to the drum while the two lengths were wound in opposite directions. The pull of the heavier driving weight turns the drum and a driving force is transmitted to the train of wheels through a pawl and ratchet. The drum of the early movements is free to rotate about the great wheel arbor but in later wood movements the drum is fixed to the arbor and it is the great wheel that is free to turn. The drum continues to rotate and the driving weight line slowly unwinds. At the same time the other line carrying the lighter weight is being wound onto the drum. When the driving weight has reached its limit of descent, the line carrying the lighter weight is fully wound onto the drum. Winding is accomplished by pulling down on the lighter weight and turning the drum in the opposite direction, free from the influence of the ratchet, causing the driving weight line to be rewound onto the drum and raising the driving weight to commence a new cycle of operation.

With such an arrangement one would not expect to find holes in the dial for inserting a key.

WEIGHTS. These were made in a variety of shapes, sizes, poundage and materials depending on the type of clock case, type of movement, and the cost of the finished clock. The shape and size was governed principally by the amount of space available to the weight. The line of descent must be free from obstruction. They must not rub against the case; they must be clear of the pendulum in all relative positions; they must not foul other lines or be so close as to touch other weights.

The amount of poundage is that which is required to overcome the frictional resistance of a clean and oiled train of wheels plus a few extra ounces to overcome subsequent additional resistance caused by thickening of oil through age.

The materials from which weights were made depended largely on cost. The cheapest were cans made from tinned iron sheet and filled with stones or sand. Probably the most used were made of cast iron, while expensive clocks frequently had weights of lead encased in brass.

Through the passage of time many old clocks have lost their original weights for one reason or another and replacement weights have been fitted which are unsuitable. Watching their descent will show whether or not they operate free from obstruction. The required poundage can be checked by hanging a suitable container and filling it with stones until the train of wheels functions with a strong action. Remove the container and stones and weigh them. To this weight add another ten ounces and this should be sufficient to operate the train. Bear in mind that a

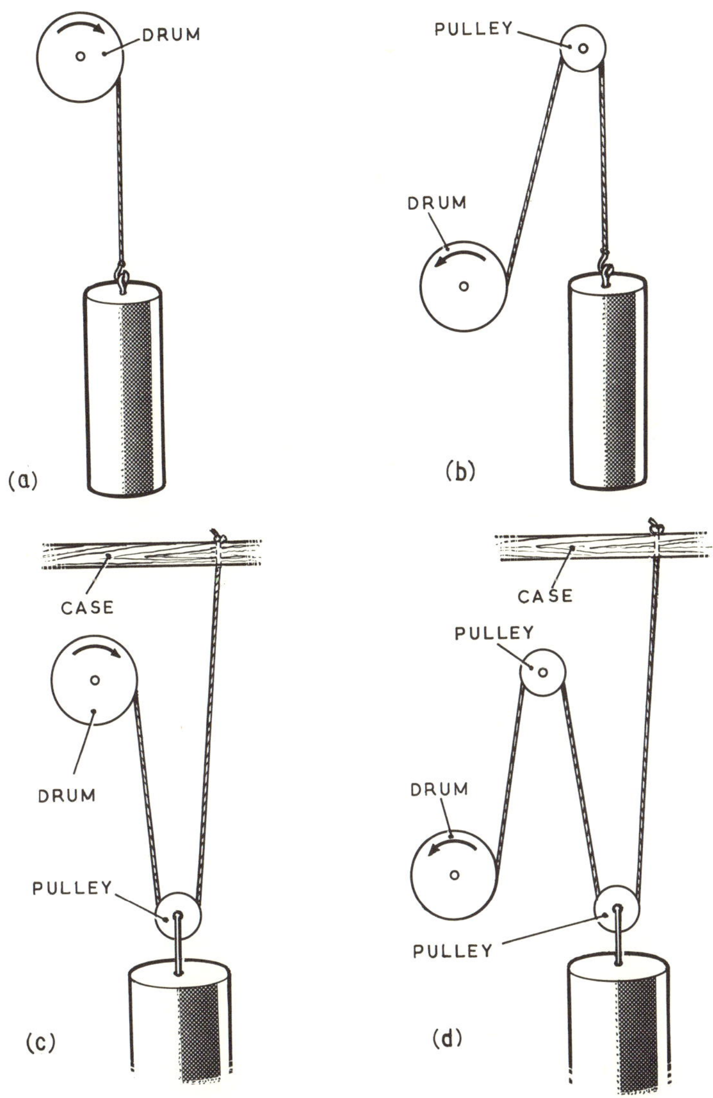

Figure 64. Lines and Weights.

weight that is too heavy will increase the rate of wear between pivots and pivot holes.

Count Wheel or Locking Plate Strike

Fig. 65 shows a side view of a typical count wheel strike mechanism without the operating levers, and Fig. 66 is a diagrammatic sketch of the strike function. The layout varied among makers and with types of movements but the general principle remained the same.

Mounted between the two movement plates are three arbors, A, B and C. Rigidly attached to these arbors are a number of levers. Arbor A carries D, E and F; arbor B carries G and H, while arbor C carries hammer tail I.

A weight suspended from the great wheel drum provides the motive power, while pin J, inserted in the face of the center wheel, starts the mechanism in motion.

The time train wheel must rotate once in each hour. Shortly before the hour is due to be struck, pin J begins to raise lever G and, because it is mounted on the same arbor, lever H is also raised. Lever F is pushed upward by lever H causing lever E to be raised clear of the hoop on the hoop wheel. At the same time, lever D is raised partially clear of the slot in the count wheel.

Now that lever E is clear of the slot in the hoop, the strike train is free to run under the influence of the weight but pin K on the warning wheel is quickly arrested by the end of lever H. This brief but audible run is known as the warning and is the partial unlocking of the strike mechanism in readiness for its release at the precise moment required.

Pin J continues to lift lever G, raising still further the other levers on arbors A and B, and lifting lever D clear of the slot in the count wheel, until the pin moves out of contact. Levers G and H drop to their former positions but levers on arbor A are prevented from so doing by lever E dropping onto the periphery of the hoop, the hoop wheel having moved around and taking the slot out of alignment with the lever end. At this moment the strike is due. When lever H drops, it swings clear of pin K, thus leaving the strike train free to run.

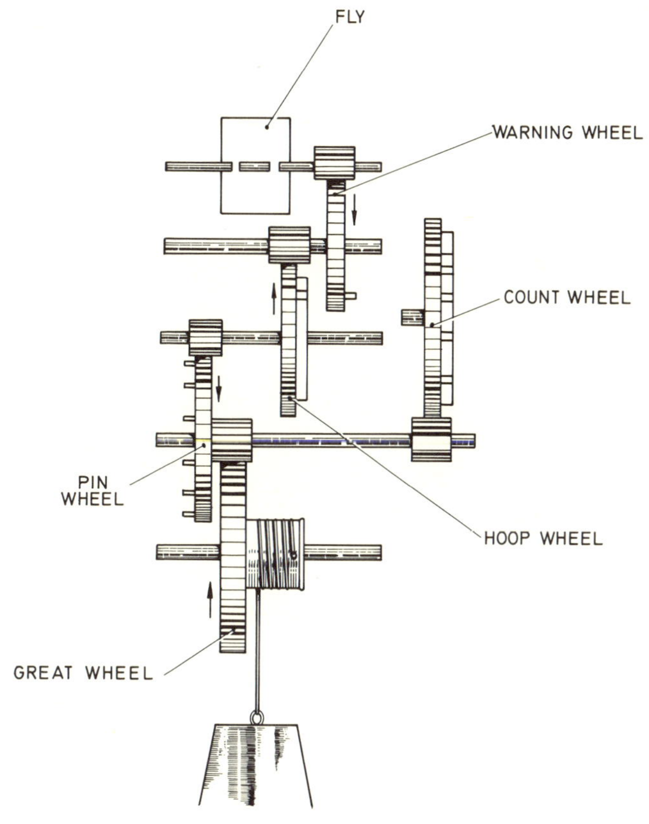

Figure 65. Count Wheel Strike Layout.

One of a series of pins, spread equidistant around the edge of the pin wheel, engages the hammer tail, causing the hammer to strike.

Striking will continue as long as lever E is held clear of the slot in the hoop. After the first stroke the hoop wheel completes one revolution and the slot is again brought in line with the end of lever E. The lever is prevented from dropping into the slot and bringing striking to a halt by the end of lever D, which has dropped onto a sector of the count wheel instead of into a slot, the count wheel having moved around a little.

The strike train continues to run and the pin wheel continues to activate the hammer as long as the end of lever D remains on the sector of the count wheel. The length of each sector determines the number of strokes of the hammer, Fig. 67, the last stroke occuring when the end of lever D drops into the next succeeding slot. When this occurs, lever E drops into the hoop slot and the strike train is brought to rest.

The distance between each pair of slots in the count wheel has to be progressively greater to allow an extra strike for each successive hour up to twelve. The exception is when the clock strikes one. In this instance lever D is raised, the hammer strikes, and the lever falls back into the same slot.

The number of blows struck by the hammer is progressive with each release of the strike train, and it is not possible for any strike to be repeated.

If the strike train is allowed to run down completely, and the time train continues to function, the hands become out of coincidence with the count wheel. To prevent this the strike train must be kept wound.

If the time train runs down, and the hands have to be reset, it is necessary that the clock be allowed to strike fully when each hour position is reached. If the hands are moved too quickly and taken beyond the strike position, then the count wheel and the hands become out of coincidence.

Whenever it is necessary to restore the correct relationship between hands and count wheel, the lever D has to be raised manually by pulling on resetting wire L and then released to allow

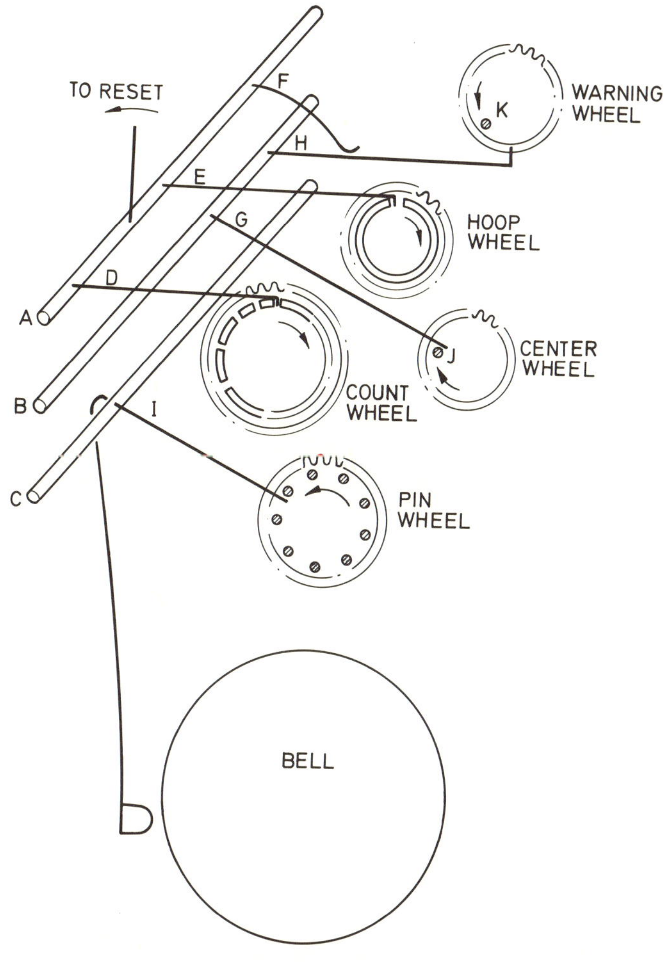

Figure 66. Count Wheel Strike Operation

the strike mechanism to function through its normal cycle. This process is repeated until the hour struck is coincident with the position of the hands.

Pendulums and Wheel Counts

In the year 1581 Galileo, the Italian astronomer, became aware

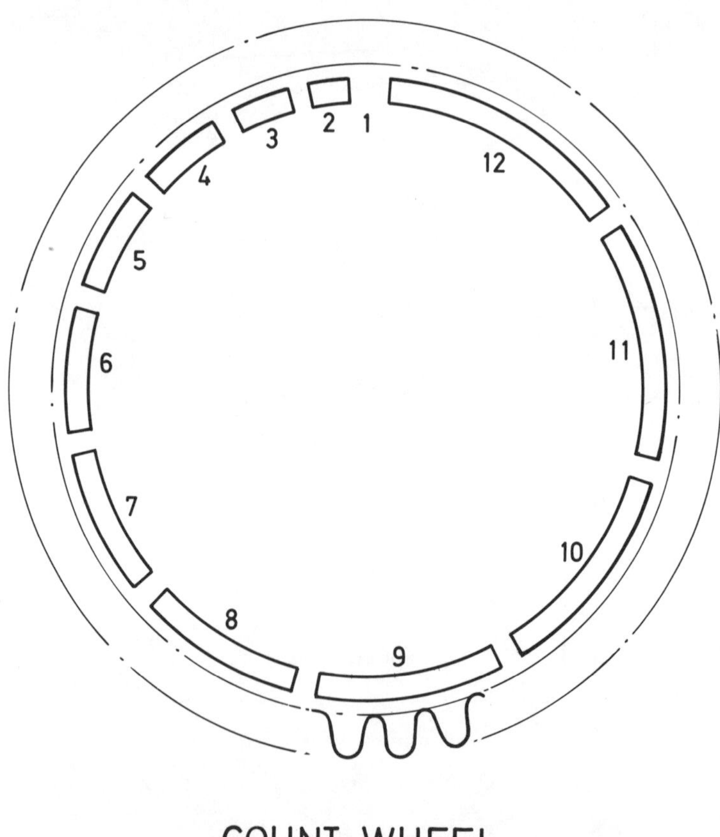

Figure 67. Count Wheel.

of a phenomenon when watching a lamp swinging from a long chain in Pisa Cathedral. He noticed that the time taken for a pendulum to complete a swing was always the same regardless of the angle of swing; it swung slowly through a narrow angle and fast through a wide angle. He also found that by increasing the length of the pendulum the time taken to complete a swing was increased and when the length was reduced, the reverse took place.

In 1657 Christiaan Huygens, the Dutch scientist and astronomer, applied these discoveries to a clock. The result was an amazing improvement, and for the first time in the history of horology a mechanical device had been made that was capable of giving near accurate timekeeping.

If a small piece of lead about the size of an orange pit is suspended from a length of thread about thirty-nine inches long, and the other end of the thread is attached to something rigid, it will be found that if the weight is allowed to swing it will take approximately one second to travel from one end of the swing to the other. Such a pendulum is said to have a rating of one second and is known as a one-second pendulum.

The point at which the thread is suspended is known as the center of suspension, and the center of gravity of the lead weight is known as the center of oscillation. Mathematicians have calculated that to make this simple pendulum swing from one side to the other in exactly one second, the distance between the center of suspension and the center of oscillation has to be 39.1393 inches.

The time taken for a pendulum to swing from one side to the other is proportional to the square root of its length as shown in the following table:

SWING IN SECONDS	LENGTH IN INCHES	SQUARE ROOT OF LENGTH
¼	2.4462	1.564
½	9.7848	3.128
1	39.1393	6.256
1¼	61.1550	7.820
1½	88.0632	9.384
2	156.5570	12.512

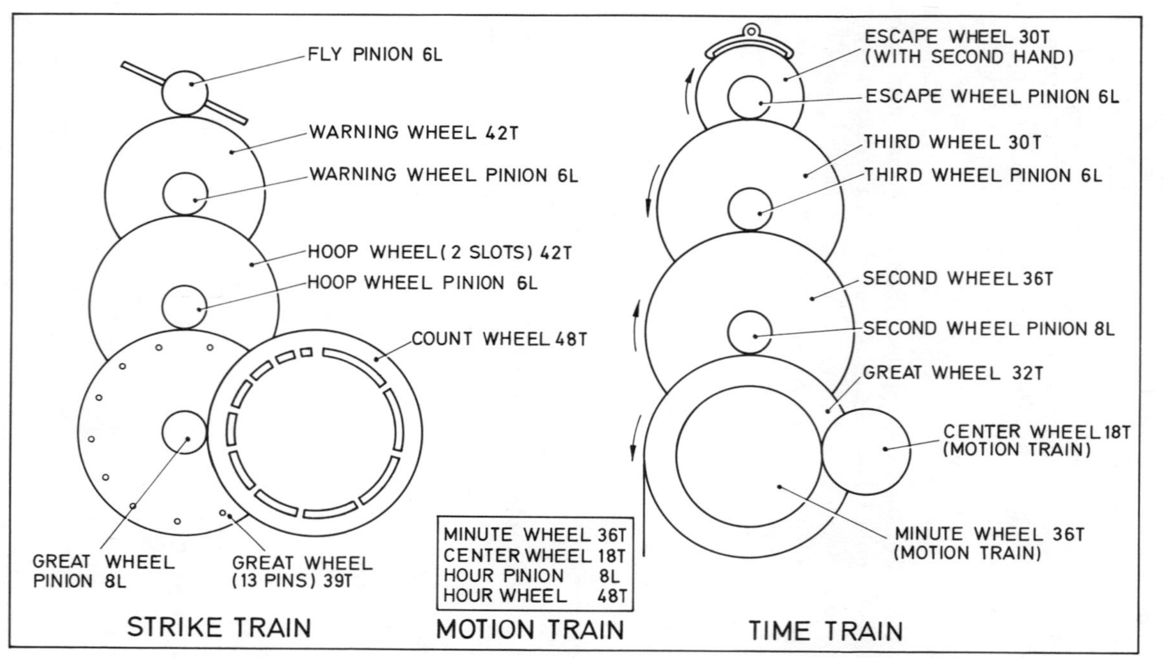

Figure 68. Wheel Counts. Eli Terry's 30-hour Tall Case Wood Movement. Circa 1802.

By moving the weight above or below the original position of the center of oscillation by means of the rating nut, Fig. 63, we vary the time taken to complete a swing. If the weight is raised, the rate of vibration is increased and the time taken to complete a swing becomes less than one second. The movement runs faster. If the weight is lowered, the reverse effect takes place.

It is not unusual to find an old clock without its pendulum and the first step towards obtaining a replacement is to calculate the theoretical length. This is done by first calculating the time train count, *i.e.* the number of vibrations the pendulum is required to make in a given time, and then apply the result to the formula

$$1 = \frac{\text{Secs. pend. length} \times (\text{secs. pend. vib./min.})^2}{(\text{replacement pend. vib./min.})^2}$$

To calculate the count we commence with the center wheel, that being the wheel that usually drives the minute hand, we count the number of teeth, multiply by the number of teeth in subsequent wheels; and twice the number of teeth in the escape wheel, and divide by the number of leaves in the third and subsequent pinions. We must multiply the number of teeth in the escape wheel by two because each tooth acts on the two pallets separately, moves the lever twice, and causes two beats of the pendulum.

Consider Fig. 68 with the following train:

center wheel	18
minute wheel	36
great wheel	32
2nd pinion	8
2nd wheel	36
3rd pinion	6
3rd wheel	30
escape pinion	6
escape wheel	30

The count is 18/36 × 32/8 × 36/6 × 30/6 × 30 × 2 = 3600 beats/hour
= 3600/(60 × 60) = 1 beat/second

We already know that the length of a pendulum with a rate of 1 beat/sec. is almost 39.14 inches and so there is no need to continue calculations by applying the formula.

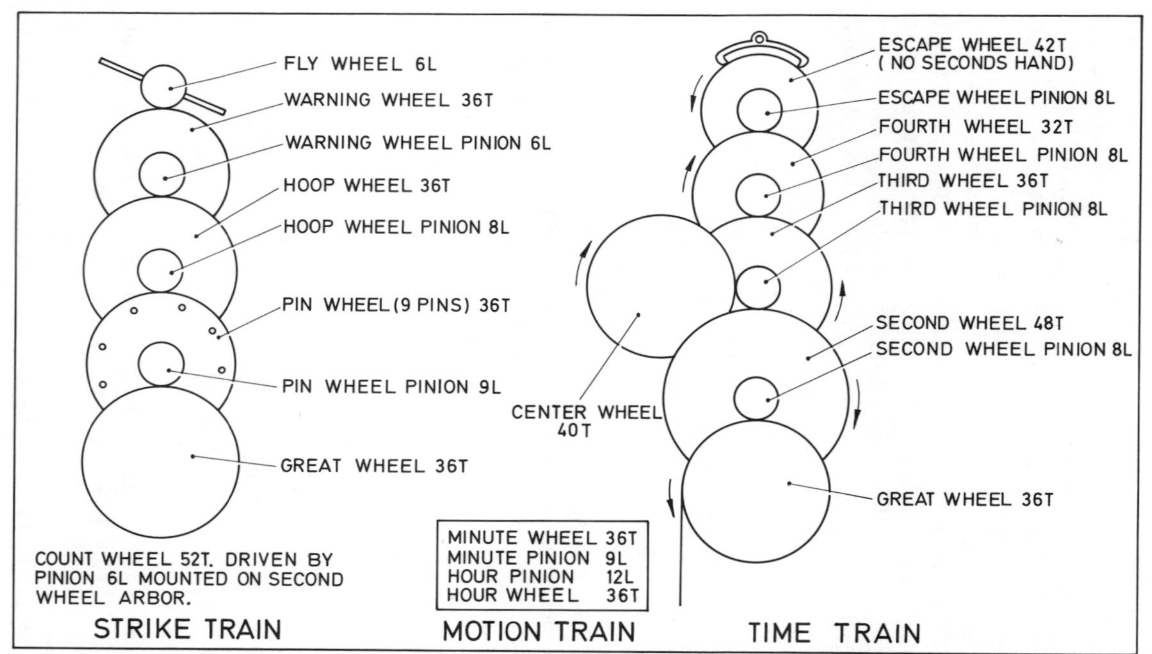

Figure 69. Wheel Counts. Eli Terry's 30-hour 5 Wheel Wood Movement. Patent 1823.

Consider Fig. 69 where the situation is different. For the purpose of the count the time train consists of:

center wheel	40
3rd pinion	8
3rd wheel	36
4th pinion	8
4th wheel	32
escape pinion	8
escape wheel	42

The time train count is therefore expressed as:

$$40/8 \times 36/8 \times 32/8 \times 42 \times 2 = 7560 \text{ beats/hour}$$
$$= 7560/60 = 126 \text{ beats/minute}$$

Now if we apply the formula we have

$$l = \frac{39.14 \times (60 \times 60)}{126 \times 126} = 8.875 \text{ inches}$$

It must be remembered that this length is the theoretical distance between the center of suspension and the center of oscillation. The actual length of the pendulum will be longer, possibly as much as an inch, depending on the weight and shape of the bob and the weight of the rod.

Anchor Escapement

This invention is generally attributed to Dr. Robert Hooke but believed to have been used first by William Clement of London about 1671. It requires very little angular movement of efficient operation, less than five degrees in fact, which means that the pendulum is also limited to the same small amount of movement. This has the advantage of being able to use a long pendulum with a one second rating, which gives greatly improved timekeeping over the half-second short bob pendulum.

The driving power in the train tries to turn the escape wheel in the direction indicated by the arrow in Fig. 70. Tooth (d) presses on the curved face of the entry pallet (f) and lifts it, causing the anchor to rock about its fulcrum.

The anchor is secured to an arbor which also carries a crutch, and therefore all three pieces must move together as an assembly. The crutch cannot move without taking the pendulum rod with it and so when tooth (d) causes pallet (f) to lift, the pendulum must swing.

At the same time that pallet (f) is raised, pallet (a) is lowered in front of tooth (c). The anchor continues to rock until tooth (d) escapes and then the wheel rotates further until tooth (c) drops onto the curved face of pallet (a).

Before tooth (c) can exercise any influence over the anchor, the pendulum continues to swing in the original direction until its inertia is exhausted. This causes slightly further lowering of pallet (a), the curved surface of which presses against tooth (c) and pushes the wheel backward giving it recoil. Tooth (c) then takes over and raises pallet (a) which causes the pendulum to swing in the reverse direction. When pallet (a) is high enough to permit tooth (c) to escape, tooth (e) will drop onto pallet (f) giving the pallet an impulse and the cycle begins again.

It is the slight reverse motion of the escape wheel each time a pallet drops that makes the anchor escapement a recoil escapement. This backward movement can often be seen on the seconds hand of a grandfather clock.

With each swing of the pendulum the escape wheel is allowed to rotate half the distance between a pair of teeth.

Fig. 71 shows a strip pallet anchor. It is a strip of steel bent to the same angles as the solid pallet and functions in the same way, but it is cheaper to produce.

Rack and Snall Strike

A strike mechanism has a train of its own and is independently powered by its own weight or spring. Nevertheless, the strike train is controlled by the time train in that once every hour a pin in the face of the center wheel raises a lever in the strike mechanism, and when the lever falls the strike train is released.

The speed at which a strike, chime or musical train is allowed to run must be controlled, otherwise the weight will fall quickly causing the hammers to function rapidly. The necessary braking effect is accomplished by fitting a small fan, known as a fly, at the

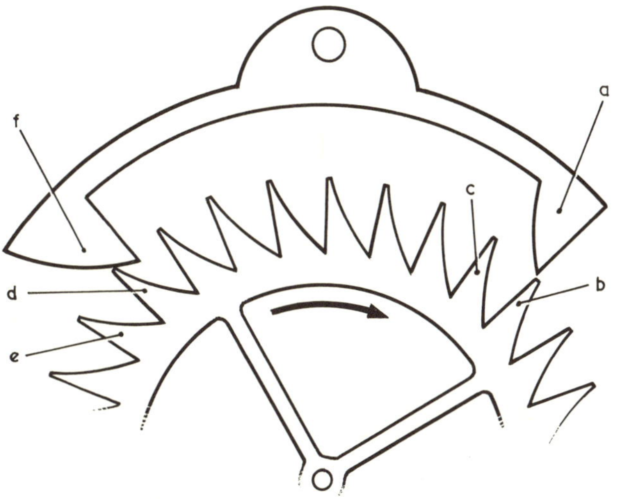

Figure 70. Anchor Escapement. Solid Pallet.

Figure 71. Anchor Escapement. Strip Pallet.

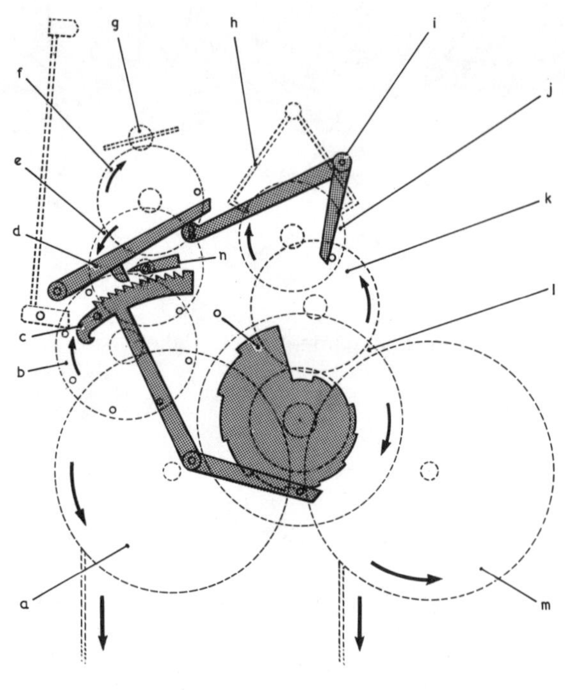

Figure 72. Rack and Snail Strike Mechanism.

end of the train. In this position, the fly is driven at high speed and the resultant air resistance is sufficient to produce the required steadying effect.

Fig. 72 shows a rack strike mechanism about to strike six. Shortly before the hour is due to be struck, the third wheel (k) of the time train has moved around and the pin is pushing against the lower arm of the lifting piece (i). The upper arm of the lifting piece has raised the rack hook (d) clear of the ratchet teeth in rack (c) allowing the rack to swing counterclockwise. The pin in the lower arm of the rack is arrested by snail (o). The snail is a flat plate with a series of twelve progressive cams cut in its periphery; the deepest cam allows the hammer to strike twelve times and the highest cam allows the hammer to function once only.

Until now the strike train has been prevented from moving by the tail of the gathering pallet (n) resting against the pin in the rack, but when the rack swings away from the gathering pallet, the strike train is released and able to rotate. Further raising of the lifting piece will place the warning piece, fixed in the end of the upper arm, in the path of the oncoming pin in the warning wheel (f) and thc strikc train will again be arrested. This initial but brief run of the strike train is known as the warning.

Exactly on the hour, the pin in the third wheel (k) will pass and release the lifting piece which will swing counterclockwise taking with it the warning piece away from the pin in the warning wheel (f). The strike train will then be free to run until the strike has been completed.

When the pin wheel (b) rotates, the pins will operate the bell hammer. At the same time, the pallet wheel (e) will rotate carrying with it the gathering pallet (n) which will gather the rack one tooth for each strike of the hammer. When the last tooth has been gathered, the tail of the gathering pallet will again be arrested by the pin in the rack and the strike train will come to rest.

The fly (g) acts as a governor and generally controls the regularity of the hammer blows. The greater the surface area of the fly, and the higher the speed of rotation, the greater will be the air resistance. Such an arrangement will produce slow hammer movements causing the bell to ring with a mature mellow sound.

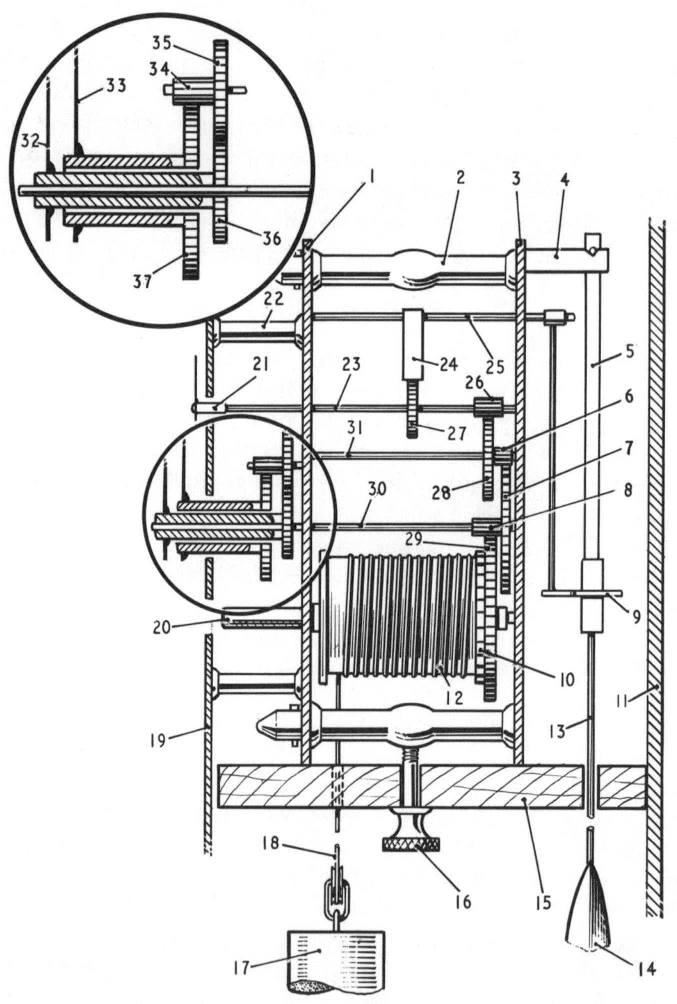
35
34
33
32
36
37
1
2
3
4
22
5
21
23
24
25
26
6
27
31
7
28
30
8
29
9
20
10
12
11
13
19
18
16
15
17
14

Figure 73.

Eight Day Brass Movement

When viewed from the front the time train is on the right-hand side of the movement and the strike train is on the left. Fig. 73 shows the time train of a typical tall case clock movement.

Weight lines are gut or stranded wire. One end is attached to the drum by passing it through a small hole provided and tying a knot on the inner end. The other end of the line passes through an opening in the seat board, around the weight pulley and back up through a small hole in the seat board. The line is then knotted to prevent it from being pulled through. If the hole is too large to hold a knot then tie a small metal bar on the end of the line. If the return hole is correctly positioned the weights will lower with the face of the pulleys parallel to the trunk door and twisting will not occur. The line must not rub against the seat board. It is bad practice to attach the line to a hook screwed into the underface of the board. The pulley can become damaged if it should be allowed to strike the hook at the completion of winding and the burr thus formed might chafe the line.

(Left)

Figure 73. 8-day brass movement. Time and motion trains.

1. front plate
2. plate pillar
3. back plate
4. pendulum cock
5. pendulum spring
6. third wheel pinion
7. center wheel
8. center wheel pinion
9. crutch fork
10. ratchet
11. backboard
12. drum
13. pendulum rod
14. pendulum bob
15. seat board
16. seat board screw
17. weight
18. line
19. dial
20. drum arbor (winding end)
21. seconds hand
22. dial pillar
23. escape wheel arbor
24. anchor
25. anchor arbor
26. escape wheel pinion
27. escape wheel
28. third wheel
29. main wheel
30. center wheel arbor
31. third wheel arbor
32. minute hand
33. hour hand
34. minute wheel pinion
35. minute wheel
36. cannon pinion
37. hour wheel

The drum and the ratchet are secured to the barrel arbor but the main wheel is free to turn about the arbor. On the face of the main wheel is a click which engages the ratchet teeth under pressure from a spring. When the winding key is placed over the drum arbor and turned in a clockwise direction, the drum and ratchet rotate and the line is wound around the drum. During this operation, it is essential that the trunk door be kept open so that the rise of the weight can be watched. If the weight is taken too high and the pulley is allowed to hit the under surface of the seat board, the shock could easily snap the line. The weight would then fall to the bottom causing damage to the case and making it necessary to repair or renew the line. When the drum and ratchet are turned the click rides the ratchet teeth, but when winding stops and the weight tries to turn the drum and ratchet in the opposite direction, the click spring holds the click into the ratchet and the power is transmitted to the main wheel.

The weights are usually made of cast iron, but in high quality clocks lead was frequently used and housed in polished brass cylindrical containers. The poundage varies from 12 lbs. to 14 lbs.

When the weight is in suspension, power is transmitted from the main wheel to the center wheel pinion and then from wheel to pinion in succession until it reaches the escape wheel, the last in the train. The anchor, which is immediately above, is so positioned that its pallets interrupt the path of the escape wheel teeth and prevent the escape wheel from rotating freely.

When the pendulum swings, the anchor is caused to rock, thus releasing one tooth of the escape wheel. When the pendulum swings in the opposite direction another tooth is released. The escape wheel delivers an impulse to the anchor each time a tooth pushes against the face of a pallet and it is this impulse that maintains the swinging motion of the pendulum, Fig 70.

The number of teeth in each wheel and the number of leaves in each pinion govern the gear ratio between each pair of wheels. The main wheel of an eight-day clock fitted with a one-seconds pendulum rotates once in twelve hours, the center wheel once each hour, the third wheel once in seven and one-half minutes, and lastly the escape wheel once every minute. The center wheel is used to drive the minute hand while the escape wheel drives the seconds hand. The center wheel also drives the hour hand by means of a group of wheels known as dial wheels or motion work which have a gear ratio of twelve to one, Fig. 73 (inset).

Maintaining Power

When the key of a weight driven clock is placed over the square of the time train drum arbor and turned, the drum rotates and the line is wound. The instant the drum is rotated in this reverse direction the motive power provided by the weight is removed from the train of wheels. Instead of the escape wheel providing impetus to the pendulum through the pallets of the anchor, the momentum in the pendulum turns the escape wheel in the reverse direction. When a seconds hand is fitted, the hand will turn counter-clockwise.

The temporary loss of power to the time train prevents the hands recording so that when winding is complete and normal running of the movement is resumed, the hands will indicate an incorrect time which can be corrected only by resetting the hands.

To prevent loss of recorded time during winding, a form of maintaining power was invented by the famous English horologist John Harrison in 1726, Figs. 74 and 75. It is known as Harrison's maintaining spring. The drum and ratchet are fixed to the arbor while the going ratchet and the great wheel are both free to turn about the arbor.

During normal running the weight causes the drum and ratchet to rotate which in turn drives the going ratchet through a click. The going ratchet turns the great wheel by compressing the maintaining spring, one end of which is located on the going ratchet and the other end is attached to the great wheel.

When the motive power is removed during winding, the going ratchet is prevented from turning backwards by the great wheel click and so the compressed maintaining spring releases its energy by driving the great wheel. This auxiliary drive lasts long enough to cover the period required for normal winding.

This refinement in timekeeping was not usual in low priced clocks; it was generally confined to regulators and the more expensive brass, eight-day, tall case clocks. The principle of operation is still used in regulators today.

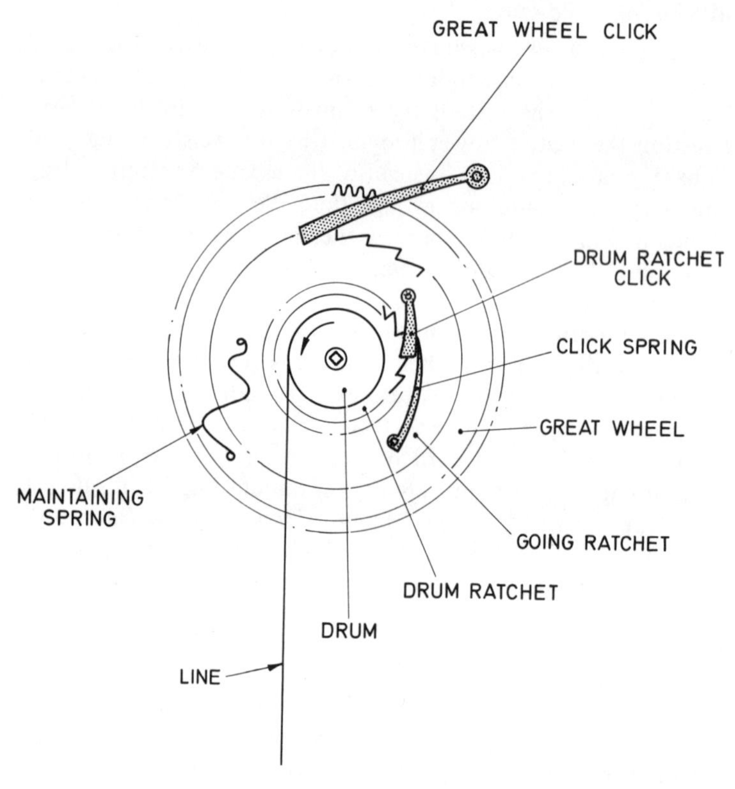

Figure 74. Harrison's Maintaining Spring. Front view.

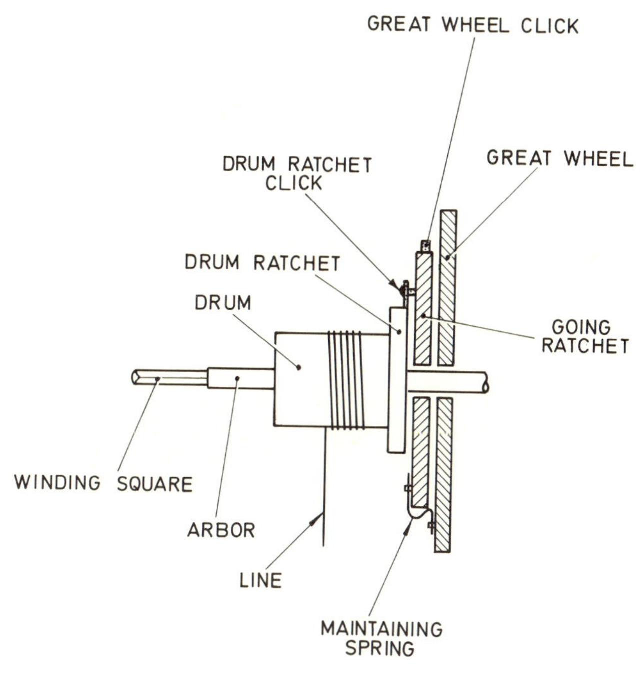

Figure 75. Harrison's Maintaining Spring. Side view.

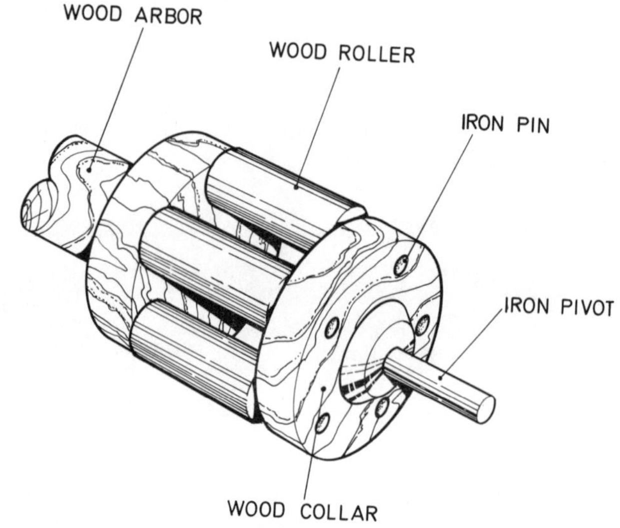

Figure 76. Joseph Ives' Roller Pinion.

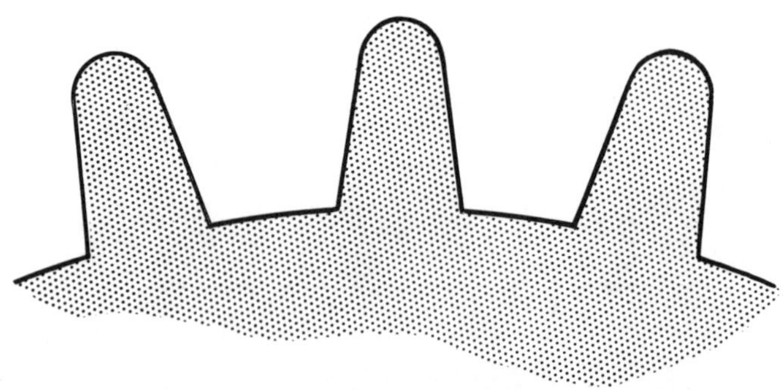

Figure 77. Wheel Teeth Used With Roller Pinions.

Roller Pinions

Joseph Ives introduced roller pinions, Fig. 76. The design was based on medieval lantern pinions that used iron pins between two plates. Ives replaced the pins with rollers and the effect was to reduce friction.

The roller pinions fitted to his thirty-hour wood movements were made of wood, whereas those fitted to eight-day brass movements had brass collars and iron rollers.

The use of roller pinions meant that wheels could no longer be cut with conventional shaped teeth; they had to be cut as shown in Fig. 77, and more widely spaced.

Dead Beat Escapement, Fig. 78

This was one of George Graham's inventions and it first appeared at the beginning of the eighteenth century in England. The principle of operation is almost identical to the anchor

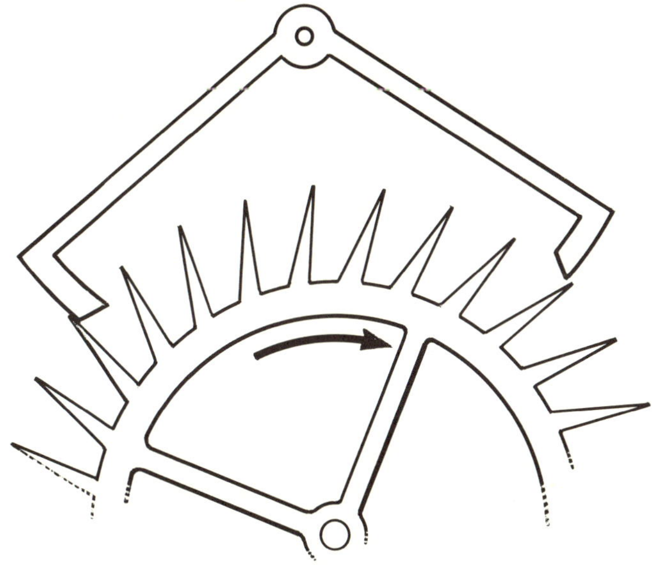

Figure 78. Dead Beat Escapement.

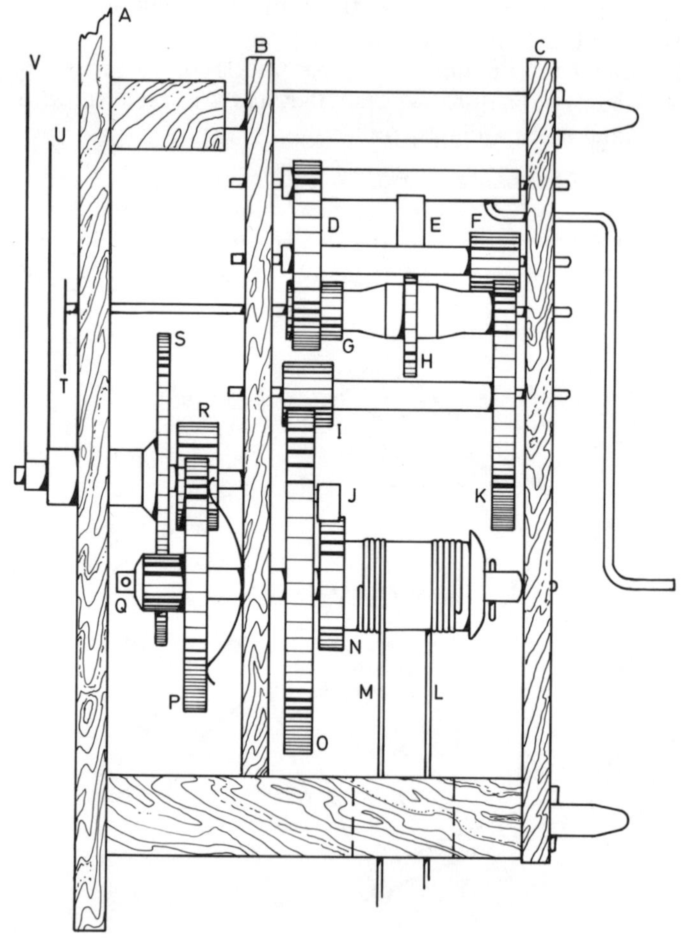

Figure 79.

escapement but the shape of the mating faces on the pallets and the teeth of the escape wheel are such that there is no recoil action.

In its original form, the pallets of this escapement spanned fifteen teeth of the escape wheel. This was later reduced to ten teeth which proved very successful when used in regulators and with weight driven movements having a one seconds pendulum. It is only in recent years that clocks in any quantity have been made with escapements having eight teeth embraced by the pallets.

The escapement requires the pendulum to be in good beat and the operating faces must be clean and free from gummy oil. If these two precautions are observed, then this escapement is capable of greater timekeeping accuracy than the anchor escapement.

Thirty Hour Wood Movement

Figs. 79 and 80 illustrate a typical layout of the time train and motion train of a thirty-hour wood movement with pull-up wind fitted to early nineteenth century tall case clocks and hang-up (wag-on-wall) clocks. The wheels and pinions of the time and strike trains are fixed to their arbors which are mounted between two wood plates, while the motion train is positioned between the movement front plate and the dial plate. The following table shows the number of wheel teeth and pinion leaves involved in the time and motion trains and the resultant gear ratios.

(Left)

Figure 79. 30-hour wood movement. Time and motion trains.

A Dial plate
B Front plate
C Rear plate
D 3rd wheel
E Anchor
F 3rd pinion
G Escape pinion
H Escape wheel
I 2nd pinion
J Ratchet pawl
K 2nd wheel
L Driving line
M Winding line
N Ratchet wheel
O Grt. wheel
P Minute wheel
Q Hour pinion
R Minute pinion or center wheel
S Hour wheel
T Seconds hand
U Hour hand
V Minute hand

TIME TRAIN

WHEEL/PINION	TEETH/LEAVES	GEAR RATIO
Great wheel	32	4:1
2nd wheel pinion	8	
2nd wheel	36	6:1
3rd wheel pinion	6	
3rd wheel	30	5:1
Escape pinion	6	
		120:1

MOTION TRAIN

WHEEL/PINION	TEETH/LEAVES	GEAR RATIO
Minute wheel	36	2:1
Center wheel	18	
Hour pinion	8	6:1
Hour wheel	48	
		12:1

Motive power is supplied by a suspended weight which causes the drum to rotate. The power is transmitted to the great wheel, through a ratchet and pawl, and then on to the second wheel pinion and second wheel, to the third wheel pinion and third wheel, and to the escape wheel pinion and escape wheel. The escape wheel arbor is projected forward through a hole in the dial, and mounted on the end is a seconds hand. We therefore know that the escape wheel of this movement must rotate once in every minute. It is the function of the anchor, crutch and pendulum to ensure that this control of speed is maintained.

The hour pinion and minute wheel are mounted loosely on the great wheel arbor but they rotate with the arbor through the means of a spring-loaded friction drive. The center wheel has an extension pipe, the forward end of which carries the minute hand. This assembly fits loosely over a center arbor. The hour wheel also has a pipe and to this is fitted the hour hand. The hour wheel with its pipe fits loosely over the pipe of the center wheel.

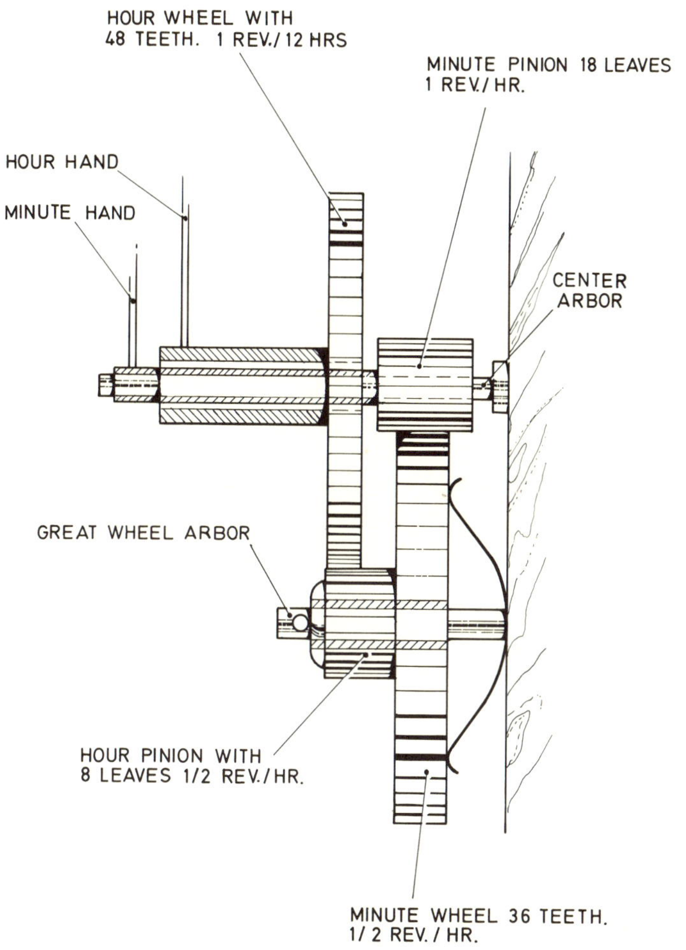

Figure 80. 30-hour Wood Movement Motion Train.

In subsequent thirty-hour wood movements, such as in Fig. 69, and almost invariably in eight-day brass movements, Fig. 73, the motion train is driven by the center wheel arbor. The gear ratio remains at 12:1.

Some movements were timepieces only, *i.e.* without strike mechanism, while others had the addition of alarm mechanism. They were also used as wag-on-wall clocks. Wood blocks were attached to the movement backplate, Fig. 81, to which a wire hanger was fitted. Plate pillars were fitted to the bottom of the movement to provide the support that would otherwise have been given by the seat board in a tall case.

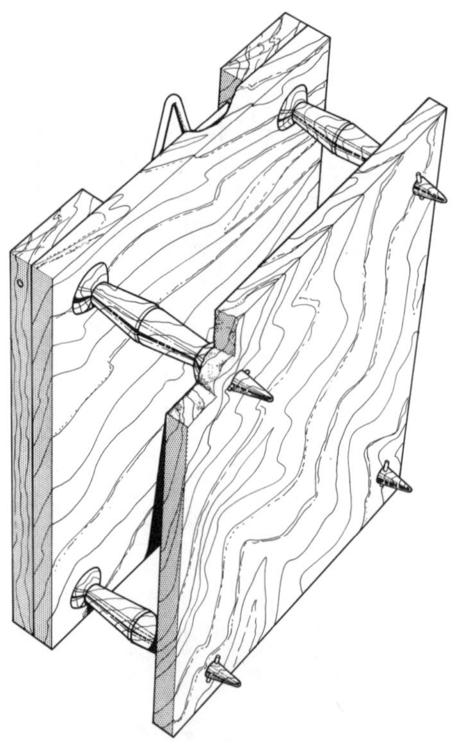

Figure 81. Hanger for 30-hour Wag-on-Wall.

Spring Motive Power

It was apparent to American clockmakers that the use of weights to drive their clocks was undesirable and that many advantages were associated with the use of coil springs as motive power. In a weight driven clock the size of the case is greatly influenced by the amount of space required by the weights, lines and pulleys. Once these have been dispensed with, the movement can be fitted into a smaller case, thereby reducing the cost and the weight of the clock and, at the same time, making it more portable.

The English had been using coil springs since 1658, when they introduced their bracket clocks, but neither the techniques of producing heat treated high carbon steel nor the production facilities were available to American makers. The cost of importing springs was not an economic proposition.

Wagon Spring

In 1825 Joseph Ives invented an ingeneous method of applying spring energy without the use of coil springs. He introduced what became known as the wagon-spring movement, which consisted of a leaf spring bolted to the bottom of the clock case that exerted a variable pull on chains, which in turn pulled on lines wound around the wheel train drums.

In Fig. 82 the device is shown in the wound position. Each end of the leaf spring is pulling downward on a yoke which engages a lever in one of a number of notches. The outer end of the lever swings about a pivot while the inner end is pulled downward, bringing with it a chain. The upper end of the chain is secured to a drum which is fitted to a pulley spindle, and when the chain is unwound the drum and pulley rotate together.

Attached to the pulley is the lower end of a line. The upper end is screwed to the drum of the wheel train and when the pulley rotates, the line is pulled and the wheel train drum turns.

By the selection of an alternative notch, the position of the yoke on the lever can be adjusted to provide an increase or decrease in the amount of pull exerted by the leaf spring.

The ingenuity of the device lay in the arrangement of the lever and chain assembly which was designed to maintain a constant torque on the wheel train and escapement and thereby insured that the pendulum swung with a regular beat.

Wagon-spring motive power was in regular use with thirty-hour and eight-day movements until about 1860. From 1844 - 1847 the firm of Birge & Fuller made large quantities of sharp Gothic clocks using the wagon spring to power their eight-day and thirty-hour movements.

Coil Spring

American made coil springs first appeared in 1836 when Joseph Shaylor Ives (not to be confused with Joseph Ives or Shaylor Ives) discovered a process of tempering springs made of brass. They were prone to breakage which frequently resulted in secondary damage, but nevertheless Elisha Brewster fitted them to his movements and sold them in large quantities to other makers who cased them under their own names.

Generally speaking coil springs were fitted to brass movements. A few were used with wood movements but they were usually experimental.

This situation continued until 1843 and then Charles Kirk invented a new type of movement back plate made of cast iron. Two circular wells were cast integral with the plate in which the two brass springs were housed. These wells prevented the springs from wandering during run down and protected the movement in the event of spring breakage.

Elisha Brewster fitted these iron back plates to his brass spring movements and they were a success. They first appeared in eight-day rack and snail movements fitted to round Gothic or beehive cases and, shortly after, he used them in thirty-hour count wheel strike sharp Gothic or steeple cases.

In 1847 Silas B. Terry claimed to have discovered a means of hardening and tempering steel springs by immersing them in hot tallow. He sold his idea to Edward L. Dunbar, a clock material supplier in Bristol, who developed the process and supplied ever increasing quantities to makers of movements. With their increased reliability they quickly replaced the brass spring.

In 1850 steel springs were operating without fusees and were being fitted direct to great wheel arbors. Even so it took another

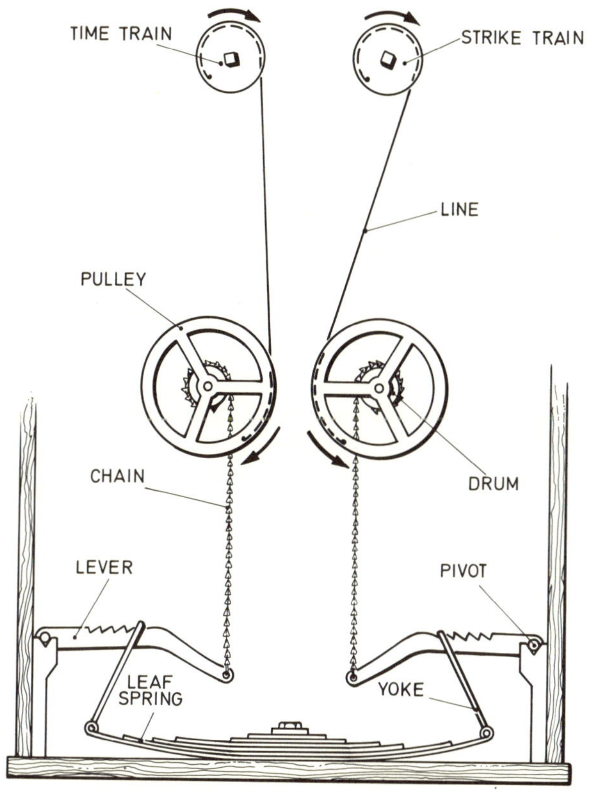

Figure 82. Wagon Spring Motive Power

fifty years of spring making experience before the quality of the steel could be said to equal that of British made springs.

The Fusee

The makers of the early Italian spring driven clocks found that whereas the mechanical energy stored in a hanging weight remained constant throughout its fall, such was not the case with a coiled spring. When a spring was fully wound it exerted maximum force, but as the spring unwound the energy contained within it became progressively less, causing the movement to slow down and lose time.

Clearly some form of compensation was required, and about 1475 the Italian clockmakers introduced a very successful device called the fusee, probably invented by Leonardo da Vinci.

Direct Fusee (English) Fig. 83

In 1658 London makers introduced the bracket clock which was motivated by the first English spring driven movement. This movement contained a fusee based on the original Italian design. The device took the form of a conically shaped pulley, with a continuous spiral groove, that was fixed to the great wheel arbor, one end of which was squared for winding. The great wheel was free to rotate around the arbor but was locked to the fusee in one direction only by a pawl and ratchet.

Parallel to the fusee was a stationary mainspring arbor carrying a winding drum that was free to rotate around the arbor. Coiled inside the drum was the mainspring, the inner end of which was anchored to the arbor while the outer end was hooked to the inner wall of the drum.

One end of a length of gut or cord was attached to the large diameter of the fusee and the other end was wound around and was attached to the winding drum.

To wind the spring a key was placed over the squared end of the great wheel arbor and turned. The fusee rotated and pulled on the gut causing the winding drum to rotate taking with it the outer end of the coiled spring. Winding continued until the gut had been transferred from the outside surface of the drum into the spiral groove of the fusee by which time the mainspring coiled inside the drum was fully wound.

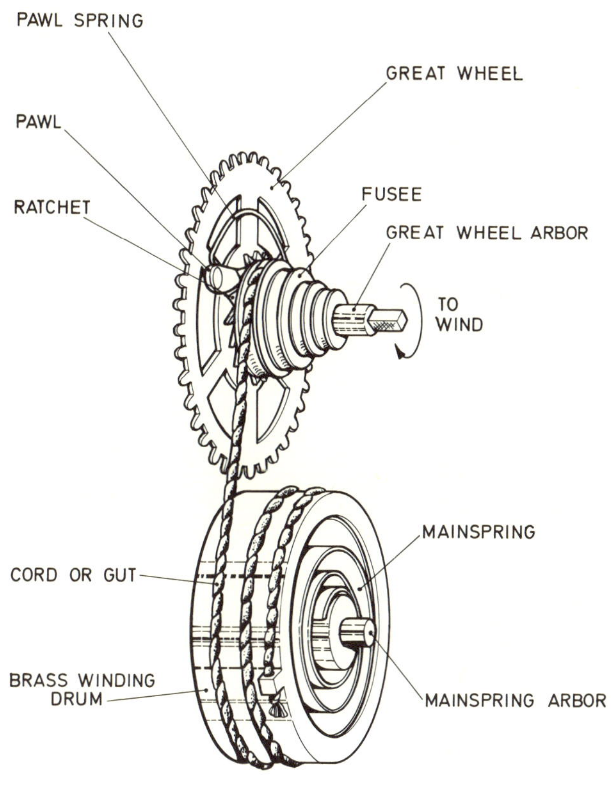

Figure 83. Direct Fusee. English.

When the key was removed the energy in the spring acted on the drum and pulled on the gut trying to turn the fusee, but the driving force was held in check by a pawl and ratchet which transferred the energy through the great wheel to the time train.

During the normal run down of the spring the drum slowly rotated and transferred back to itself the gut line from the fusee. In so doing the gut pulled on the fusee on a progressively reduced diameter, thereby increasing the leverage and maintaining a constant torque. This counteracted the loss of energy within the spring. To accomplish this the fusee had to be made to the correct shape and size.

Reverse Fusee (American) Fig. 84

In 1840 Charles Kirk designed a new form of fusee that became known as the reverse fusee. The following year E. C. Brewster introduced a new style of clock known as the round Gothic or beehive. The case was designed by Elias Ingraham, and E. C. Brewster produced them with an eight-day brass movement driven by a brass coil spring with Kirk's fusee.

By 1847 steel springs were becoming more readily available in America and there began a rapid change from weight driven to spring driven clocks. The use of a reverse fusee detached from the movement enabled existing weight driven movements and those in current production to be powered by springs with little or no alteration to the movements. Many makers entered the more financially rewarding market of spring driven clocks.

The position of the fusee in relation to the movement and the method of incorporation varied considerably among makers but the principle of operation and its effect remained the same.

With a reverse fusee the winding drum was positioned on the great wheel arbor and the fusee on the mainspring arbor; the opposite was the case with a direct fusee. The gut line was attached to the fusee at its largest diameter, wound into the spiral groove and from the smallest diameter led away to the winding drum

When the winding drum was turned by a key placed over the squared end of the great wheel arbor, the gut was pulled and the fusee and mainspring arbor turned taking with them the inner end of the mainspring which was anchored to the arbor. The outer end

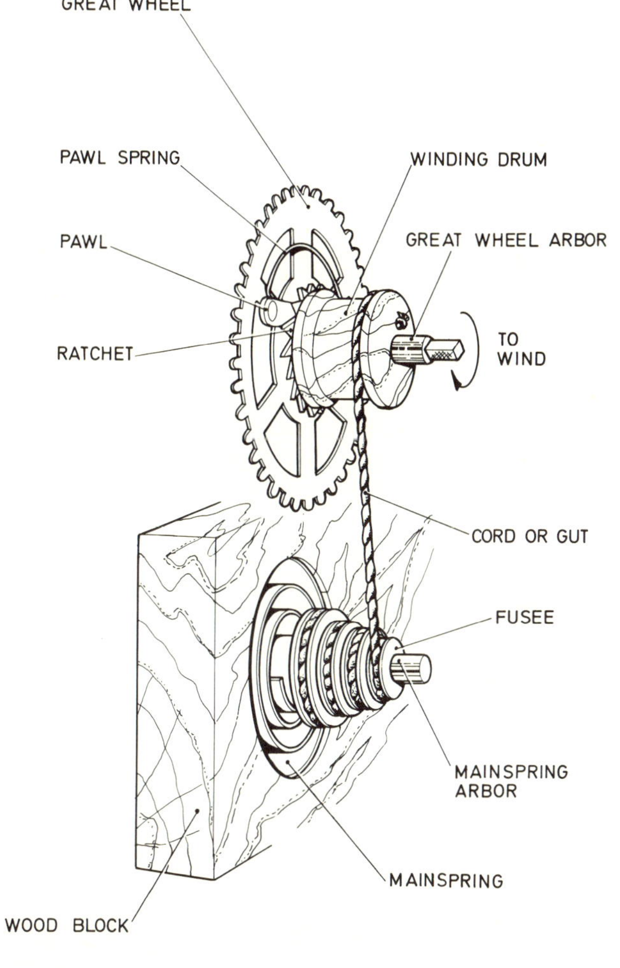

Figure 84. Reverse Fusee. American.

of the mainspring was held stationary and therefore the rotation of the fusee caused the spring to be wound. By the time the gut had been transferred from the fusee to the drum the spring was fully wound.

After winding, the spring was prevented from rapid unwinding by the pawl and ratchet that locked together the drum and the great wheel. During normal unwinding, the gut is first pulled by the largest diameter of the fusee and as the energy within the spring decreases so does the effective diameter of the fusee until, when the spring is nearly run down, it is the smallest diameter that is effective. By this means a constant torque on the drum is maintained.

The fusee of the reverse type rotates at the same speed as the mainspring arbor whereas this is not the case with the direct type. It is principally for this reason that the shapes of the two fusees have to differ.

The springs of early reverse fusees were usually housed in wood blocks secured to the back of the case beneath the movement and frequently close to the floor of the case. In 1846, many clocks were made with the springs and fusees mounted in light iron or brass frames and the springs contained in barrels. The frames were screwed to the backs of cases anywhere from the floor to a position immediately beneath the movement.

Chauncey Boardman and Joseph A. Wells conceived the idea of riveting brass extension arms to the bottom corners of the movement plates so that they formed a framework immediately beneath the movement in which the spring and fusee units were located. On New Year's Day in 1847 they were granted a patent.

This arrangement was followed by movements being made with these extension pieces integral with the plates. The final change was to embody the fusees within the movement and thus dispense with the need for extension arms to the plates.

Chiming and Musical Arrangements

Very few clocks with chime or musical arrangements were made prior to about 1855. They were fitted with a cylinder or barrel which is mounted horizontally between the movement plates. The cylinder has a large number of short pins fitted to its outer surface, and as it rotates the pins actuate the hammer tails of up to about eleven bells.

Tall case clocks are invariably fitted with subsidiary dials in the lunette so that control of chimes and tunes is possible. The tune selector consists of a pointer that is manually turned within its own dial upon which is painted up to about seven tune titles. When selection is made the cylinder is moved along its own axis, thereby offering a different set of pins to the hammer tails. Other controls sometimes fitted in the lunette are Strike-Silent, Chime-Silent and Music-Silent, all of which provide the owner of the clock with full control of all audible arrangements.

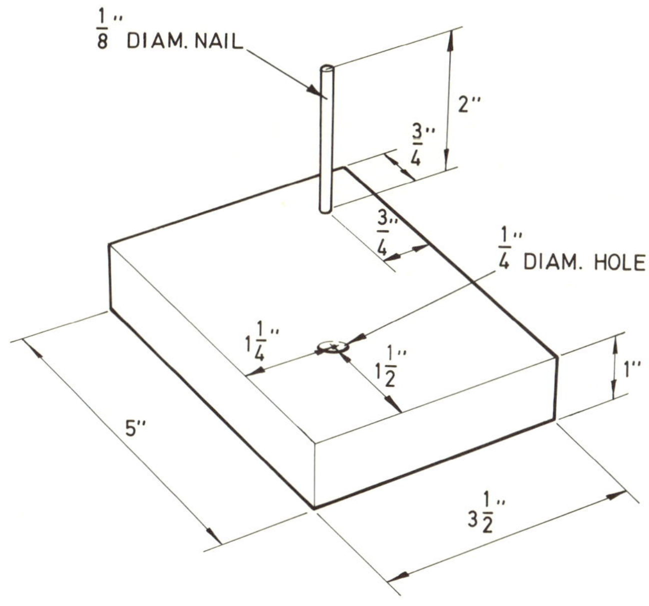

Figure 85. Home Made Spring Winder.

Tin Plate Movement

In 1859 Joseph Ives was granted a patent for his invention of a low priced eight-day coil spring movement with strike using heavy gauge tinned iron sheet for the plates and wheels.

The movement plates were discs and to increase their rigidity Ives introduced circular ribs by rolling. The wheels were cut from the same material by conventional methods. Friction was kept to a minimum by running arbor pivots in brass bushes held in the plates, by using roller pinions in brass collets throughout, and by using a squirrel-cage type of rolling escapement instead of the usual escape wheel. Fusees were sometimes fitted.

Wood blocks were used to hold the movements to the backs of the cases. The pendulum was hung in front of the front plate and the crutch was cranked to provide clearance for the center arbor during swing.

These movements were fitted into wood shelf cases from 1859 until about 1865 by several Bristol makers, the most notable being N. D. Brewster, E. & A. Ingrahams and E. Ingraham & Co. Beehive clocks with these movements fitted were not made in large numbers, and those that have survived are rare.

CHAPTER 6

Restoration of Cases

Renovating a Wood Case

REMOVE THE PENDULUM and, if the movement is weight driven, lift out the weights. Remove the door, glass tablet if fitted, hinges, catch, lock and any metal ornamentation. Then unscrew and lift out the movement.

Inspect the case for joints and blocks that need regluing and damaged or missing veneer, molding and feet. Some moldings and feet can be obtained from suppliers of clock material. Screws that are loose in their holes can be tightened by inserting wood plugs. One or more broken pieces of matchstick will often be sufficient. Make a note of the materials likely to be needed. Members of the National Association of Watch and Clock Collectors, Inc. receive regular copies of Mart in which suppliers of materials advertise. These advertisements are instructive and at the same time provide a mail order service that in some circumstances might well be the only convenient method of obtaining materials.

Veneering a Complete Panel

The majority of clock cases were made of pine, because of low cost, and then covered with a thin veneer of hardwood, usually mahogany with some maple, rosewood and walnut. If the veneer is extensively damaged or most of it is missing, it is better to start again rather than attempt a repair. If only slight damage has been sustained or a small piece has come away and been lost, then usually a repair is all that is needed.

To re-veneer a complete panel, the remains of the old veneer must be removed. This is best done by ironing with a hot clothes iron. Keep the iron clean by placing a sheet of paper over the work. If heat will not soften the glue, try dampening with water after first scraping away any protective coating from the veneer. During the process of dampening the veneer, take care to prevent the rest of the case from becoming unnecessarily wet.

With all the veneer removed the wood surface will carry some of the original glue, probably in patches. This is not a good surface on which to fix new veneer. Wrap a piece of coarse sandpaper around a sanding block or rubbing block, preferably of cork, and rub the surface until it is reasonably flat. A little care is needed to prevent rounding at the edges and corners.

The old method of gluing wood was by applying hot animal glue, made from fish or bone, to both surfaces and holding them together until the glue was cold and hard. The process was rather laborious and a little messy. It had one advantage as far as veneering is concerned in that a flat iron, standing in boiling water, could be applied to the veneer and the heat would be sufficient to soften the glue allowing repositioning or complete removal.

Modern techniques favor the use of contact adhesive. The adhesive takes the form of a jelly and is applied to both surfaces and allowed to dry. The two surfaces are then brought together with slight pressure and adhesion is almost instantaneous. It will be seen that this method makes no allowance for error, but if the veneer to be applied is cut a little larger than the panel to be covered, then the edges can be trimmed, thus dispensing with the need for accurate positioning.

There is, of course, no reason why one of the wood glues currently available should not be used. In this event, the veneer will need to be kept pressed to the wood over the entire area by weights or clamps until the glue is set.

Most hardwood suppliers keep a stock of wood veneers and will most likely be able to supply associated materials such as stains and polishes.

It is sometimes helpful to cut a thin card pattern to the shape required. Lay the pattern on the veneer and mark in pencil on the face the part that is to be exposed. Remove the pattern and place the veneer on a flat cutting surface. A piece of vinyl sheet used for floor covering is ideal for absorbing the knife cuts. Use a small craft knife with detachable sharp pointed blade. When the cutting edge has been blunted, the blade can be discarded and a new blade fitted. Use a steel rule to guide the knife blade and cut one eighth of an inch outside the pencil lines for trimming. When cutting along the grain there may be a tendency for the grain to steer the point of the knife. Make a number of light strokes in preference to completing the cut in one stroke. Repeat the same cutting technique across the grain; this will reduce splintering of the veneer along the cut edge. Turn the veneer over, apply the glue to both mating surfaces and position the veneer onto the wood face. If a contact adhesive is being used allow both surfaces to dry completely.

When the veneer is fixed, turn the work over so that the veneered panel is on the cutting surface and trim away the surplus. Keep the knife as upright as possible to prevent the cut being made at an angle and apply the knife in a series of light strokes. The veneer is now ready for smoothing and polishing but first it is advisable to experiment on a test piece.

To veneer a curved surface use a thin veneer if available. A contact adhesive is more satisfactory for this operation than the use of wood glue. Cut the veneer to shape, apply the adhesive to both surfaces and wait until it is thoroughly dry. Soak the veneer in water which will enable it to be shaped without fracture to the fibers. Remove water moisture from the adhesive with a dry cloth and apply the veneer to the curved surface, starting at one end.

When wood is subjected to long exposure the surface color darkens; it is a natural process known as patination. The color has to be matched when finishing the new veneer. When polish is applied to wood the surface color is darkened immediately. An even darker color can be obtained by first applying stain to the veneer.

Take a piece of veneer and glue it to a piece of flat wood. Smooth the surface by rubbing it lightly with a piece of very fine sandpaper wrapped around a rubbing block. Rubbing must always be done with the grain. To rub sandpaper across the grain produces scratch marks which are visible through the polish. Thoroughly brush away all powder and dust.

The veneer is now ready to receive the lacquer. The old method of finishing was to apply French polish, a mixture of shellac and methylated spirit or alcohol, by means of a cotton pad. Many applications were made building up into a film thick enough to produce a gloss finish. As with gluing, techniques in polishing have changed. The modern method is to use transparent lacquer sealer or polyurethane varnish which is applied by brush. This lacquer is available in a number of brands and full instructions for its use are given with each. Lay the clock case so that the area to be lacquered is horizontal . This will allow the lacquer to flow evenly and eliminate runs.

Go through the stages of applying the lacquer to part of the test piece and compare the result with the rest of the clock case. If the color is too light, apply some stain to an untouched area of the test piece, and when dry, coat it with lacquer as before. The instructions with the lacquer will recommend the type of stain to be used. It will usually have spirit base.

Repairing Old Veneer

To cut and insert a small piece of new veneer is not difficult but, as with completely re-veneering a panel, some trial and error mixed with patience and careful handling is necessary.

When gluing new veneer alongside the original veneer the butt joint that runs with the grain is not noticeable. The same cannot be said about mating edges that have been cut across the grain. It is, therefore, better to cut and lift a complete strip of the original veneer that runs with the grain and is as wide as the area to be repaired. If this is not practical or desirable, then the edge of the original veneer surrounding the exposed wood must be trimmed back to a uniform shape to which the new veneer must be cut.

Take a piece of veneer larger than is required, and by rubbing it with sandpaper wrapped around a rubbing block, reduce its thickness below that of the original veneer. This is to allow for the build-up of lacquer.

Care must be exercised in cutting the veneer patch because it must fit exactly. To help in this respect place a length of Scotch tape over the edges to be cut. The tape will hold the wood fibers together during the cutting process. By selection, choose a piece that will match the original grain as nearly as possible.

To reglue veneer that has lifted as a blister, cut the blister in the center along the grain with a safety razor blade and insert wood glue with the point of the cutting knife. Apply a little pressure until set. If the veneer has lifted at the edge of the panel, raise the veneer with the point of a pin and insert wood glue. The procedure for polishing is as previously described.

Refinishing

A clock case whose veneer is intact but whose finish is dirty and scratched can be restored with little trouble. All that is required is that the outer film be removed. With it will go the dirt and most of the scratches.

Wrap a piece of No. 360 wet and dry paper around a rubbing block and rub with the grain. Keep the paper wet by frequent dipping in water and periodically wipe the work for inspection.

When the rubbing down process is complete the surface must be clean and dry. A coat of finishing lacquer is then applied and any hairline cracks will be filled and not seen.

Sometimes one finds a clock with a relatively undamaged case but which has been given a thick coat of varnish that has dried leaving brush marks. The most satisfactory method of producing a good finish is to remove the varnish and start again. On flat surfaces the varnish can be removed by scraping, using a carpenter's scraper and wood chisel.

When molding or carving are involved then a solvent will be required and applied by a stiff brush. Experiment first with methylated spirit or alcohol. If this is found to be unsuitable, try a mixture of turpentine or white spirit with an equal quantity of household ammonia. If neither of these fluids produce a successful result, a varnish remover will have to be applied. For this purpose it is better to use a remover that can be killed by spirit in preference to a remover that has to be washed away by water. Follow the manufacturer's instructions; they will most probably include precautions to be taken in respect to skin irritation, protection to eyes, inflammability and adequate ventilation.

Overwetting exposed veneer may soften the glue causing the veneer to lift. If pressure is applied to the veneer while drying takes place the veneer will reglue itself. When dry, rub down to a smooth surface and apply lacquer as previously described.

Cleaning Metal Parts

Metal parts were usually given a thin film of laquer to maintain their brightness and preserve them against corrosion caused by moisture and chemicals in the air. With age the protective film will, in all probability, have become damaged and the exposed metal surface will have suffered accordingly.

Remove the lacquer by soaking in methylated spirit or varnish remover and rub away any stained areas with very fine emery paper. Polishing is best done with a coarse metal polish. Brass finials are best polished in the revolving chuck of a lathe or vertical drilling machine. The finished surface is then given a thin film of lacquer, an excellent method of application being by spray.

Gold Leaf

This is the process of applying gold leaf to an adhesive surface of gold size. The gold leaf is supplied in small book form, each leaf being exceedingly thin and fragile and supported and protected by tissue. The gold leaf is available in three weights: 16 karat (pale gold), 18 karat (yellow gold) and 23 karat (deep gold).

It is unlikely that all the gold leaf will need replacing; it is more usual to renew missing or badly damaged areas. Carefully scrape away the damaged leaf with a pointed cutting knife and clean the exposed surface by lightly rubbing with a soft cloth moistened in methylated spirits. Take care not to disturb the surrounding gold leaf.

Apply a thin film of gold size to the selected area, very slightly overlapping the surrounding gold, and wait for it to become tacky. In the meantime, with a pair of small sharp scissors, cut a piece of gold leaf slightly larger than the exposed area.

Small pieces of gold leaf are picked up by a special gold leaf brush which has to be charged with static electricity. The charge is introduced by passing the hairs of the brush across one's clothing or through one's hair. Too big a charge will cause the brush hairs to snatch the gold leaf rendering handling almost impossible.

With the correct amount of static electricity the brush hairs will pick up the gold leaf without damage and allow the leaf to be positioned on the work. During this operation do not breath on the gold leaf, as it may be blown away.

Place a piece of paper over the new piece of gold leaf and, with the tip of one finger, gently press the leaf onto the surface. Continue this process until all damaged areas have been repaired.

Renovating Clock Papers

Clock manufacturers used thin glue to secure their clock papers or labels to the backs of cases. With age both paper and glue become brittle causing the paper to separate from the glue in patches. It is necessary that these papers be preserved as much as possible because, without them, much of the identity and possibly value of the clock is lost.

Lay the empty case on its back and carefully ease back the clock paper thus exposing the glue, most of which will be on the case and possibly a little on the back of the paper. Flatten the glued surface on the case by rubbing with a coarse sandpaper and brush away the dust. Paint the area with diluted wood glue and gently ease the clock paper back into position carefully pressing it down with a cloth pad using a dabbing action.

Black Iron Cases

Black enameled cast iron cases are frequently found with chipped enamel and with rust on the exposed metal surface. It is very probable that the original paint was baked on, in which case it would be extremely difficult to remove the enamel. By far the most practical method of renovation is to refinish the damaged areas only.

Scrape away any rust and clean the metal by rubbing with a medium grade emery paper at the same time producing a beveled edge to the surrounding enamel. Brush on a coat of rust inhibitor in accordance with manufacturer's instructions and leave to dry.

Position the clock case so that the area to be treated is uppermost. Build up to the required thickness by applying successive coats of black brushing cellulose making sure that each coat is dry before applying the next.

The original enamel will have lost its high gloss through age and to obtain a matching surface some of the gloss must be removed from the new enamel. This can be accomplished by rubbing with a paste of fine pumice powder and water.

Dials

Three types of dials will be encountered among nineteenth century clocks: enamel, paint and paper. Enamel was the most expensive and usually the most pleasing in appearance. Paper was the cheapest; they were printed in quantity, whereas painted dials were individually produced by hand.

Enamel Dials

The enamel or porcelain was fired onto an iron or copper plate at high temperature. The finished surface is hard and brittle and has no flexibility. An old dial is frequently crazed with minute hairline cracks and only by raising the temperature of the dial to near the melting point of the porcelain can these cracks be removed. Such a temperature would destroy the numerals and any painted decoration. It follows that nothing can be done in this respect and one has to accept the cracks.

Missing pieces and chips are a different matter. If the metal plate has been exposed it must be scratched or scraped clean, and the edge of the surrounding porcelain must be beveled with a small piece of medium grade wet and dry paper. The area from which the porcelain is missing can now be restored by applying successive layers of pure white acrylic paint. This is a household product sold for retouching chips in domestic appliances such as refrigerators and sinks. It is applied by a pencil brush. When dry another coat is applied building up until the level is slightly above the dial surface. The repair is then reduced by a dead smooth file until it is level with the surrounding porcelain and finally polished by rubbing with a soft cloth dipped in an abrasive fluid such as metal polish used on brassware.

Painted Dials

Painted dials are made of wood or metal. If the damage is minor then restoration can be carried out by local retouching. If damage to the face is extensive then complete repainting may be necessary. Usually there is sufficient outline of the numerals and decorative designs to make this possible. Use black Indian ink or artists' copying ink for the numerals and artists' oil colors for the decorations. The oil colors are available in convenient small tubes in a wide range of colors.

The most satisfactory result is achieved by making a new dial plate and spraying it with off-white cellulose paint from an aerosol can. The numerals and decorations are then copied from the original. Drill the center hole when the painting is finished. This will enable a pencil compass to be used for marking the chapter rings between which the chapters or numerals will be painted. The center of the dial will also be required for penciling the radii that will represent the minute markings in the minute ring and for marking the positions of the numerals. Rings can be drawn by using an ink compass.

Paper Dails

Printed paper dials are glued to wood or metal dial plates. Unless the damage is slight, in which case local retouching is all that is required, it is better to remove the paper dial and glue a new one in its place. There are many suppliers of clock materials that can offer a wide range of printed paper dials. It will be necessary to supply them with dimensions and to state whether Roman or Arabic numerals are required.

If the original dial has colored designs these can be copied onto the new dial using colored inks; different shades can be obtained by mixing. In this event, the original dial must be retained. It can be removed by using the steam from a boiling kettle.

Old glue is removed from the dial plate by rubbing with coarse sandpaper and metal plates are finished by rubbing with steel wool. Apply an even coat of wood glue to a wood plate and lay the paper dial in position. Remove any air bubbles by smoothing out from the center. Use the same technique with a metal plate but apply a contact adhesive to the metal only and position the paper dial immediately while the adhesive is still wet.

When the work is thoroughly dry, dial holes can be cut with a sharp pointed cutting knife and colored inks can be applied if required.

RESTORERS AND SUPPLIERS OF MATERIALS AND TOOLS

Case Repairs and Restoration
Bruce C. DeGrange, Antique Imports, 125 East St., Frederick, MD 21701

Clock Case Glasses
Horace E. Holder, A.A. Glass Service, 1001 9th St. No., St. Petersburg, FL 33701

Dials Replaced or Restored
Bruce C. DeGrange, Antique Imports, 125 East St., Frederick, MD 21701
Susan S. Bearden, 1651 S.E. Lava Drive (Suite 5), Milwaukie, OR 97222
TEC Specialists, P.O. Box 909, Smyrna, GA 30081
Judith W. Akey, 55 Beaver Dam Road, Scituate, MA 02066
Stanley Maxwell, 51 Brooklawn Place, Bridgeport, CT 06604

Gold Leaf and Artist Materials
Carson & Ellis, 1153 Warwick Avenue, Warwick, RI 02888
Charette Corp., 31 Olympia Avenue, Woburn, MA 01810
Lambert Co., Inc., 920 Commonwealth Avenue, Boston, MA 02215
Talas, 104 Fifth Avenue, New York, NY 10011

Movement Repairs and New Parts Made
John Winen, P.O. Box 312, Sunnymead, CA 92388
R. Givler, 146 3rd Street, Box 9, Wadsworth, OH 44281
Frank W. Fulkerson, 4141 Monroe St.,Toledo, OH 43606
Ken Leeseberg, Ken-Way, Inc., 311 Chestnut St., Addison, IL 60101

Repair and Replacement Bronze, China and Porcelain Case Ornaments
Mort Jacobs, Whippie Street, Chicago, IL 60645

Reverse Painting
Mrs Irene B. Worthy, 200 Polk Avenue, Dallas, GA 30132
Emily Anderson, P.O. Box 631, Santa Monica, CA 90406
Tom Moberg, 115 S. Howell St., Owosso, MI 48867
Cindy Burleigh, Gilders Workshop, 7 Sheffield Rd., Winchester Rd., MA 01890
Nateli Stoddard, Shawenon Studio, North Egremont, MA 01252

Tools, Materials and Movement Parts
S. LaRose, Inc., 237 Commerce Place, Greensboro, NC 27420
Clock Repair Center, 220-17 Jamaica Avenue, Queens Village, NY 11428
Tiny Clock Shop, 1354 Old Northern Boulevard, Roslyn, NY 11576

Wheel Cutting and Repivoting
J.C. VanDyke, 1039 Rt. 163, Oakdale, CT 06370
Carl Nisson, Nisson Clock Wheel Co., 3220 South St., Redding, CA 96001
H.G. Swisher, 2117 Monticello, Lakeland, FL 33801

Wood Case Parts
Harry Warner, 109 Pine Cone Court, Ellettsville, IN 47429

Wood Veneers
Thomas Adamson, 51 Carmel Avenue, Salinas, CA 93901

CHAPTER 7

Preservation of Movements

Preliminary Inspection

SOME NINETEENTH CENTURY movements are well over one hundred years old. Every moving part will show signs of wear and if all those parts were to be replaced by new ones, always assuming they were available, the original movement would cease to exist and its antiquity would be lost. Some collectors consider that if a movement is so badly worn that only extensive replacements will enable it to run, then it might be better to leave it alone and retain its originality.

It follows that preservation of an old movement is best confined to cleaning, repair of broken parts, renewal of any missing pieces and adjustment.

If a movement appears to be reasonably clean, runs well and keeps good time, there is little to be achieved from interfering. Movements that run badly or fail to run at all are the ones that need attention.

When a movement is in its case the extent to which it can be inspected is limited. It is well worth the time and trouble making a simple wood stand. This will enable a preliminary inspection to be carried out with considerably more freedom. The movement can be more readily observed and adjustments more easily made before it is returned to its case.

The design of a stand suitable for weight driven movements usually takes the form of a stool with an open top. If the movement is screwed to the back of its case the stand will require fitting with an upright piece of wood for the same purpose. When drilling the holes for the movement fixing screws make sure they are so positioned that the movement will be vertical and not leaning slightly to one side.

Remove the hands and lift off the weights and pendulum. Remove the movement from its case and fit it to the stand for inspection; it is possible that the fault may be of such a nature that correction can be carried out without disassembly. Remove any fluff or particles of dirt with a small brush and make sure there are no missing parts. Hang the time weight, suspend the pendulum and set the movement in motion. If the pendulum is out of beat place some packing material underneath one side of the stand until a steady tic-toc is heard. If the movement stops restart it and pull gently downward on the weight line to increase the driving force. If the movement then continues to run it probably means that the movement is in need of cleaning or adjustment.

Fit the hands. Lift off the time weight and hang the strike weight. Turn the minute hand in a clockwise direction and study the operation of the strike mechanism. Make notes and sketches to show the location of each wheel and pinion of both trains and the position of the warning and locking levers and pins. This information will greatly facilitate assembly.

Before the movement can be disassembled, and to complete the preliminary inspection, the driving force must be removed. Lift off the weights or let down the mainsprings, whichever is appropriate. Springs must first be fully wound and then a clamp or retainer is fitted around them. These clamps are lengths of steel rod shaped as a letter C identical to those already in position when a new spring is purchased.

Mainsprings are very powerful and could cause personal injury to hand or fingers if allowed to run down out of control. It would also most probably result in damage to the spring or adjacent parts. Make sure that the movement is secure, that the key will not slip in your hand and that the click can be released immediately at any time. A simple but effective tool can be made from a few inches of wood broom handle with a slot cut in one end into which the flat of the winding key is a push fit. Turn the key in the direction of winding to remove the pressure from the click. With a small screwdriver lift the click clear of the ratchet and allow the spring to unwind slowly keeping it under control with hand pressure. When the spring has expanded into the clamp the key may be withdrawn.

With the driving force removed from the wheel trains an assessment of the amount of wear between pivots and pivot holes can be made. Hold each arbor between finger and thumb, or if out of reach use long tweezers, and move each pivot from side to side in its hole. Any that are worn to excess will need attention. Keep a record of these. This inspection will reveal any broken pivots.

If lantern pinions are fitted, give consideration to the possibility of moving the pinion further along its arbor to a new position which will enable an unworn area of the pinion to be offered to the teeth of the driving wheel.

Disassembly

A wooden box, a small drawer or a stout cardboard box without a lid will make a suitable stand upon which to lay the movement. Have the bottom edge of the plates nearest you and proceed as follows:

1. Remove all parts outside the plates.
2. Withdraw taper pins from front end of plate pillars.
3. Carefully lift off front plate.
4. Remove all components. Separate time from strike by placing them in separate boxes. Identify each wheel by marking in pencil on the front face. Mark the cord drums to indicate which is time and which is strike.
5. Remove mainspring from clamp. Make up a simple tool as shown in Fig. 85. Insert the arbor of the wheel and spring assembly into the hole and place the loop at the outer end of the spring over the nail. Hold the wood block in a vice, wind up the spring with the broom handle and key, remove the clamp and slowly unwind the spring. The wheel with its arbor can then be removed from the spring.

Cleaning

Most of the cleaning is done by washing. Pivot holes in plates are cleaned with pegwood sticks and rust is removed by emery cloth. Professionals use a special cleaning fluid in a cleaning machine, but the occasional movement washing can be done with carbon tetrachloride. The work must be carried out in conditions of good ventilation and away from any form of ignition.

A seamless container is needed such as an aluminum saucepan that is no longer used for food. Pour in the carbon tetrachloride to a depth of about one inch and brush each part with a one-half inch paint brush. Metal parts may be immersed and soaked if required but do not soak any parts made of wood. After washing, lay the parts on a few sheets of absorbent paper to drain and dry and remove the container of carbon tetrachloride to a safe place and away from the work area.

Take a piece of clock repairer's pegwood stick or a toothpick, shave to a long point, insert it into a pivot hole and gently spin it between finger and thumb so that any dirt inside the hole will become embedded in the wood. Treat each pivot hole in both plates in the same way.

In these early movements, iron wire was used for making levers, detents, pins, etc. They will not withstand being bent as frequently as would steel. Rust on these pieces is best removed with smooth emery cloth moistened with a drop of light machine oil.

If rust is present on the mainsprings, it is better to replace them with new springs. Sooner or later the rust will weaken the spring to a point where it will not withstand the tension of being wound and it will snap, probably causing further damage. Immerse the spring in gasoline and brush thoroughly. Wipe both faces with a clean soft cloth starting at the inner end.

Inspection and Repair

After all parts have been cleaned they are inspected for breakage and excessive wear. When a collector is faced with repair work and he does not have access to workshop facilities, there is no alternative but to take the work to a clock repairer. Under these circumstances it is usually preferable to go to someone who specializes in old clocks.

Wear between pivots and pivot holes causes incorrect depthing of the wheel teeth and if this becomes excessive the movement will not run. All worn pivots should be renewed. This is a simple job with wood movements. Old pivots can be pulled out of their wood arbors and reversed. Failing this, new pivots can be made from a piece of pivot wire which is available from suppliers in short lengths and in a range of diameters.

Worn or broken pivots in a brass movement have to be drilled out and new pivots inserted. This operation calls for the use of a clockmaker's lathe. Pivots should be finished with a burnisher to produce a hard polished surface. Those that are slightly bent can, with care, be straightened.

When all pivots have been serviced each should be entered into its respective pivot hole and moved from side to side to assess the amount of wear. Refer to the notes made during the preliminary inspection. Situations arise where the preliminary inspection revealed some wear between a pivot and its bearing hole but subsequent replacement of the pivot has produced a satisfactory improvement. A new pivot that continues to have excessive side movement in its hole means that the plate will have to be bushed to restore the pivot hole to its original diameter. This applies to both wood and brass movements.

To bush a wood plate, either the original bush of ivory or brass must be pressed out or,if the plate was without bushing,the pivot hole must be redrilled to accept a bush. Brass bushings and brass bushing wire with various hole sizes are available from material suppliers. The new bush is pressed into positon and the pivot hole is cleaned out by inserting a reamer and spinning it between finger and thumb. The hole is then polished with a burnisher. Check the amount of clearance by holding the plate horizontally and inserting the pivot. The arbor should lean slightly away from the vertical. When carrying out this work for the first time it is advisable to practice on a piece of oak of similar thickness to that of the movement plate.

To bush a brass plate the procedure is more detailed and requires more tools. There are three methods of doing this work, each employing a different type of bush. They are known as riveted bush, friction bush and French bouchons. A full chapter is devoted to this subject in *Advanced Watch and Clock Repair.*

To replace or repair a wheel tooth in a wood movement is not difficult. When a small piece is missing it can be replaced by building up successive applications of plastic wood and then dressing back with smooth glass paper to the original size and shape.

If the damage to the tooth is extensive it is better to cut it off and fit a new one. After removing the tooth level with the base, cut a notch in the wheel roughly corresponding to the shape of the outer end of neighboring teeth. Take a piece of close grained hardwood such as cherry, the same thickness as the wheel, and shape one end to fit the notch. The grain should run with the radius of the wheel. When the glue has set, shape and smooth the inserted piece of wood to conform to the other teeth.

A damaged tooth in a brass movement can be removed down to the level of the base by using a square needle file. Then cut a groove into the wheel using a warding needle file or an equaling needle file. A short length of brass wire is then soldered into the slot and filed to the shape of neighboring teeth.

After renewing a tooth, the wheel and its arbor must be fitted between the plates, in its correct position, along with the pinion that is driven by the wheel. Apply light finger pressure to the finger arbor to act as a brake and turn the wheel in its normal direction of rotation. Study carefully the relative positions of the new tooth with the pinion leaves or wires and compare with other teeth. Correct depthing is important, and there must be no roughness or undue friction when the new tooth rolls through the pinion.

Damaged or missing wires in a lantern pinion are easily replaced by inserting a new length of pinion steel which is available from material suppliers in different diameters.

Inspect the plate pillars of a wood movement for tightness in the back plate. Any looseness should be corrected by forcing wood glue into the crack.

Disfiguring black marks can be removed from wood plates by applying wood bleach.

Iron wire levers and detents that are loose in their arbors must be tightened. First try reriveting the ends and if this is not successful a fillet of metal adhesive should be applied where the wire enters the arbor.

Assembly and Adjustment

If the movement is spring driven begin by winding the

mainsprings. Position the great wheel arbor in the center of the spring and engage the hook or pin in the hole at the inner end of the spring. The spring is soft at the end and will respond to being wrapped around the arbor.

Place the spring winder in a vice, position the arbor in the hole and the outer loop over the nail; with the broom handle and key wind up the spring until the clamp can be positioned around the spring.

The pieces that fit between the plates may now be assembled. Lay the back plate flat on the open cardboard box as before and, with the aid of sketches and notes previously made, insert the arbors making sure each pivot is placed in its correct pivot hole. Start with the time train and then the strike train. When all pieces are in position the front plate can be lowered. Careful handling is required at this stage to prevent accidental breakage to pivots.

With very light finger pressure, press down on the bottom edge of the front plate and guide the pivots into their respective pivot holes gradually working upwards towards the top edge of the plate. As the work progresses the front plate is allowed to lower itself until finally when all pivots are in position the front plate is fully home and the taper pins can be inserted in the plate pillars.

If the verge fits between the plates instead of outside, it may be helpful to wait until the front plate is almost fully home before positioning the verge.

At this stage the pivots and mainsprings of brass movements are oiled. Clock oil is supplied in small bottles and no other oil should be used. It is applied by means of an oiler which is a short length of steel wire flattened and shaped at one end with a handle at the other end. Both oil and oiler can be obtained from a clock material supplier at little cost.

Dip the oiler into the bottle and deposit the oil picked up by the oiler onto a piece of clean flat glass by holding the oiler upright and touching the end to the glass. Wipe the oiler dry and replace the cork in the bottle. Pick up a small quantity of oil by touching the oiler to the oil and transferring it to a pivot. When the end of the oiler is in contact with the pivot the oil will flow from the oiler by capillary action into the countersunk sink or well that surrounds the pivot.

Continue this process until all pivots have been oiled and then deposit two applications of oil to each mainspring by touching the edge of the spring.

Pivots of wood movements are left dry but mainsprings are oiled as previously described.

Do not oil the teeth and leaves of wheels and pinions of any clock, brass or wood. These must remain dry.

The next operation is to check the action of the strike train and to do this the movement must be positioned in its normal stance by mounting it to the wood stand.

Give the strike train some power by hanging the weight or making two or three winds on the mainspring. Fit the clock hands and turn the minute hand in its normal direction of rotation; never turn it backward.

When the hands near the hour position the strike warning system should operate and when they reach the hour position the strike should function and the correct number of hammer blows should be registered.

If the strike mechanism does not function correctly then the assembly must be checked. Refer to the notes and sketches previously made and refer to the mechanisms described and illustrated in Chapter 7. When the fault has been found it will undoubtedly mean that the plates will have to be separated and the strike components repositioned.

The action of the recoil escapement must now be checked and power must be given to the time train either by hanging the weight or by a few winds to the time mainspring.

Move the crutch slowly from side to side and observe the action of the escape wheel dropping onto the pallets and, at the same time, form an idea of the angle of swing the pendulum must make to release the escape wheel teeth.

It will be seen that deep locking will necessitate the pendulum passing through a large angle of swing which in turn demands more power. Remember also that if the pallet fails to release an escape wheel tooth just once, the movement will stop.

If, on the other hand, the depth of locking is too shallow, mislocking is likely to occur resulting in an erratic gain in timekeeping.

There are two types of pallets used, the strip pallet Fig. 71, and the solid pallet Fig. 70, both of which are provided with means of adjusting the depth of locking.

In the case of a movement fitted with a strip pallet, the holes in the pallet cock are elongated and all that has to be done is slacken off the two screws, reposition the pallet cock and tighten the screws. It is a matter of trial and error but the correct position is quickly found.

Adjusting the depth of a solid pallet is done by altering the position of a screw on top of the back plate. Slacken off the two pallet cock screws, rotate the adjusting screw and tighten the pallet cock screws. By turning the adjusting screw in a clockwise direction the pallet cock is raised which reduces the pallet depth. To increase the depth the screw must be turned counterclockwise.

Having checked and adjusted the pallet depth, we have insured that the escape wheel teeth will be properly locked. Now we can examine the amount of drop.

The drop of an escape wheel is the distance it travels from the release of a tooth from one pallet to the next arrest of a tooth by the other pallet.

To check the drop apply the same technique as was used when checking the pallet depth. The best method of determining whether the amount of drop is correct is to compare it with a similar movement that has had little wear. Make a note of the adjustments that are needed; then remove the pallet cock and lift the pallet arbor from the movement.

If the pallet is the strip type all that is needed is to bend the offending pallet or pallets. Bending the entry pallet outward will decrease the drop on that pallet and bending the exit pallet outward will increase the drop on that pallet.

These strip pallets can usually be bent cold but as a precaution against cracking it is advisable to heat them first. If the pallet faces are worn use a very smooth file to eliminate the wear, smooth off with a very fine emery stick and finish with a burnisher.

With the solid type of pallet the drop can be increased by reducing the entry faces. These pallets are too hard to file and a stone must therefore be used. An oilstone such as is used by a cabinet maker is best for this job. Make sure the stone is kept flat and that it follows the contour of the pallet.

The marks from the oilstone are then removed by an oilstone slip keeping the grain flowing with the pallet. Finish off with a very fine emery stick and then burnish.

Little can be done to decrease the drop in the solid type of pallet but this is not important. What is important is to avoid having too little drop. Such a condition can, after pivot holes are worn, lead to the pallets fouling the tops of the escape wheel teeth and stopping the movement.

One last word about checking the drop of the escape wheel. All escape wheel teeth must be checked with both entry and exit pallets. Any variations in drop on one side of the wheel to a position diametrically opposite will indicate the wheel being out of round.

When the escapement is functioning satisfactorily give some attention to the pendulum and crutch. If the pendulum spring is bent or otherwise damaged, it should be renewed. At the point where the pendulum rod passes through the loop of the crutch, the rod and inside faces of the loop should be clean and smooth. Hang the pendulum and observe the fore and aft clearance between the rod and the loop. There should be enough to ensure that the rod does not touch the ends of the loop at any time. The side clearance between the rod and the loop should be an absolute minimum. It is here that a touch of oil is required on either side.

Now that the work is finished it is advisable to give the movement a run before fitting it back into its case. A little packing may be required underneath the stand to provide a regular beat, but if the stand has to be raised noticeably on one side then the crutch will have to be bent sideways. Use two pairs of pliers. Hold the crutch about an inch from the top with one pair and with the other pair a little lower down, bend the crutch very slightly to one side. When the beat is irregular it means the pendulum is swinging a greater distance to one side than it is to the other. To correct this the crutch is bent towards the side on which the greater swing is taking place.

CHAPTER 8
Some Famous Makers

ELISHA CURTIS BREWSTER (1791 - 1880)

Elisha Brewster was born in Middletown and at the end of his schooling was apprenticed to a local clothmaker. He was never trained as a clockmaker and yet by the middle of the nineteenth century he had become one of the most successful and influential producers of clocks in Connecticut.

In his early days Elisha Brewster demonstrated his natural talent as a salesman when he was employed by Thomas Barns Jr. as a clock peddler traveling in the southern states. Perhaps his greatest contribution towards achieving a successful business career was his ability to recognize talent in others and then use their skills to the benefit of his own business.

It is likely that during the time that Brewster was peddling clocks he considered the possibility of setting himself up in business and selling his own clocks. In 1832 he purchased a complete clock workshop from Charles Kirk of Bristol and started the firm of E. C. Brewster & Co. Charles Kirk was retained and he and Joseph Shaylor Ives were employed as foremen. By the following year the company was manufacturing eight-day brass movements.

In 1836 Joseph Shaylor Ives invented the brass coiled spring and in 1840 Charles Kirk designed the reverse fusee for use with Ives' invention. Elisha Brewster wasted no time. In 1841 he was the first to produce commercially eight-day movements driven by coiled springs. They were marketed in beehive cases made by Ray & Ingraham.

Two years later Charles Kirk invented the cast iron back plate with integral spring housings for protection against damage in the event of spring breakage. Brewster immediately incorporated this new idea in subsequent movements. Such was his shrewd judgment of personal talent.

Then came the demand for new case styles, particularly for export to England. Brewster was well aware of Elias Ingraham's ability in this respect and so, in 1843, he entered into partnership with Elias and Andrew Ingraham, dissolved E.C. Brewster & Co., and formed a new firm, Brewster & Ingrahams. Elisha Brewster's son Noah L. was sent to England to represent his father's company.

In 1844 Brewster introduced the steeple case which was fitted with brass movements incorporating Kirk's cast iron back plate. The new firm then quickly took the lead in production among Bristol clock manufacturers.

Three years later Elisha Brewster suffered a setback in that Charles Kirk left the company to enter into a business partnership manufacturing musical clocks. The following year Joseph Shaylor Ives left Boston to set himself up in business manufacturing small musical organs.

In 1852 Brewster & Ingrahams was dissolved and a new firm was formed trading under the name Brewster Manufacturing Co., which included Noble Jerome as one of the partners. It was not successful and the agreement was terminated in 1854.

In 1855 Elisha Brewster entered into partnership with his son and formed E. C. Brewster & Son, after which he retired in 1859 a very wealthy man.

THE CURTIS BROTHERS

Samuel Curtis Sr., a clockmaker, and his wife Sarah, had four sons, all of whom were born in Roxbury, Massachusetts. One of Sarah's four sisters married Aaron Willard, who became uncle to the four Curtis boys. The first born was Samuel followed by Lemuel, Benjamin and Charles. Lemuel became famous as a clockmaker while his three brothers distinguished themselves as artists.

SAMUEL CURTIS (1785 - 1879)

It is not known where Samuel received his training but he was probably apprenticed to Charles Bullard, a well known Boston dial maker, who made dials for the Willards and other clockmakers.

In 1807 he entered into partnership with Spencer Nolen, another skilled dial maker in Boston, and the two men traded as Nolen & Curtis.

Samuel became a highly skilled ornamental painter. He produced looking glasses in highly decorative gilded frames with painted panels, some with side candle brackets. Others had split columns decorated with stenciled painting. His clock dials and reverse painted glass tablets were superb.

Dial plates were made of iron and painted with several coats of enamel, each being rubbed flat and smooth. Samuel's early dials were invariably painted with Arabic numerals but his later work carried Roman numerals.

In 1820 Samuel's partnership with Spencer Nolen was dissolved and he joined his brother Benjamin, but after 1824 he continued in business on his own.

About 1858 Samuel took his family to live in Burlington, Vermont, where he retired having amassed a small fortune from his delicate and colorful brush work.

LEMUEL CURTIS (1790 - 1857)

Lemuel's work as a clockmaker was consistently of a high standard. In the absence of any documentary evidence it is not unreasonable to assume he was trained by his uncle Aaron Willard.

In 1811 he moved to Concord, Massachusetts and took over shop premises. Almost immediately he began preparations for the manufacture of exact copies of his uncle's Patent Timepiece, or banjo. It was not long, however, before he began making small changes in design which, in the opinion of many collectors, improved its artistic appearance. In particular, the waist panels were made slightly narrower and the reverse paintings on the glass tablets were considerably more elaborate and decorative.

From this development of the banjo there emerged, in 1814, America's famed and most beautiful clock, the girandole. The reverse paintings on the tablets were exquisitely executed. Such titles as Shipwreck of St. Paul, Perry's Victory on Lake Erie, Commerce, Aurora with Phoebus Driving the Chariot of the Sun, and Lady of the Lake are particularly famous.

In 1816 Lemuel entered into partnership with Joseph Nye Dunning (1793 - 1841) and formed the firm Curtis & Dunning. The partners moved to Burlington, Vermont in 1818 where they operated a clockmaking business and jewelery shop. During the next fifteen years Lemuel produced gallery clocks, girandoles, large quantities of his uncle's banjo timepieces and almost as many lyre timepieces, thought by some to have been introduced by his cousin, John Sawin.

Lemuel was not a casemaker and although he designed his own clocks and timepieces he contracted the work of making cases. Much of the dial painting, reverse painting of tablets and gilding was done by his brother Benjamin.

The brass movements he made himself and fitted them to the cases. The movements were extremely well finished. Plates were hand scraped and polished and pillars were decorated with turned rings. On occasions even the wheels were engraved with some form of decoration. The finish was comparable to many French clocks of that time.

About 1824 Lemuel became involved in real estate and as time passed his involvement deepened until he found himself without capital. In 1832 the partnership was dissolved and Lemuel continued on his own but the depression of 1837 did much to damage his financial position and in 1842 he filed for bankruptcy.

BENJAMIN B. CURTIS

Benjamin was born in 1794 and, like his eldest brother Samuel, became a talented dial maker, gilder and ornamental painter. Between the years 1820 and 1824 he was in partnership with Samuel, after which he worked alone. He painted many glass tablets for Lemuel. The quality of his work was magnificent and although many samples of it carry his signature there are pieces believed to be by him that are unsigned.

CHARLES CURTIS

Charles was born in the year 1800. His artistic talents took him into the world of portraiture in which he became justly famous.

Very early in his career he did some ornamental painting on clock cases for Lemuel.

EPHRAIM DOWNS (1787 - 1860)

Ephraim Downs was born in Wilbraham, Massachusetts and at an early age his family moved to Waterbury, Connecticut. It was there that he was apprenticed to a carpenter.

It is possible that Downs may have received training in the mass production methods of wood movements from Eli Terry whose factory was in the locality.

In 1811 Downs started work with Lemuel Harrison & Co. at Waterbury making wood movements for tall case clocks. In 1814 the factory was destroyed by fire and he obtained employment with Clark, Cook & Co. of Waterbury.

In 1815 Ephraim Downs went to Ohio, Connecticut with his brother Anson, where they were employed by Read & Watson making wood movements. A few months later the firm was dissolved, but Luman Watson carried on and Downs stayed with him.

After ten years as a factory worker Ephraim Downs decided to havc his own business, and in 1821 he left Luman Watson in Ohio and moved to Plymouth, Connecticut with his brother where he started a small clock factory making tall case movements for other makers. Many of his movements were made for Silas Hoadley who, in 1822, became his brother-in-law.

Although the business was comparatively small, it was nevertheless a success and after four years of trading Ephraim Downs decided to expand. In 1825 he moved to Bristol where he purchased a grist mill and other building property from George Mitchell who bought movements and cases from others, assembled them and sold them under his own name. By 1829 Downs had supplied Mitchell with a few thousand movements most of which Mitchell fitted to pillar and scroll cases. Eli Terry was among the other makers to whom Downs supplied movements.

It seems that Ephraim Downs was on good terms with Eli Terry. This is understandable if it really was Terry who had given Downs his initial training. The outcome was that in 1830 an agreement was reached between the two men whereby Downs was allowed to manufacture movements that incorporated Terry's patents. From then until his retirement in 1844 Downs increased his range of products by purchasing cases from others and selling complete clocks to the wholesale trade. He concentrated on shelf clocks and supplied many thousands of looking glass cases and O. G. cases fitted with thirty-hour movements as well as bronzed and carved cases.

Ephraim Downs was one of the few clockmakers who survived the financial depression of 1837 and in this respect the continuance of his grist mill on a commercial basis made a valuable contribution.

When Ephraim Downs retired he leased his factory to other clockmakers.

SILAS HOADLEY (1786 - 1870)

Silas Hoadley was born in Bethany, Connecticut and after leaving school was trained as a carpenter.

In 1807 when Eli Terry entered into a contract with the Porter brothers, Silas Hoadley was one of two carpenters employed by Terry; the other man was Seth Thomas. Neither Hoadley or Thomas had any previous knowledge of clockmaking but their training with wood and how best it could be worked was the type of experience Terry required to assist him in tooling up a production line.

At the end of the contract in 1810 Terry sold his factory to his two principal employees. It says much for the instruction given and the experience gained during those three years of the Porter contract that the two men were able to qualify so remarkably in such a short time. They carried on the production of top grade wood movements for tall case clocks and hang-up clocks and traded as Thomas & Hoadley.

In 1813 Thomas sold his share of the business to Hoadley and set up business on his own. Hoadley continued with the manufacture of tall case movements until about 1825 and then started production of pillar and scroll clocks, some of which were fitted with modified Terry thirty-hour five-wheel train wood movements, while others were made with a thirty-hour wood movement of his own design. The winding drums in the latter movement were at the top and the wheel train worked downward to the escapement at the bottom. The strike hammer and bell were above the movement. This design has become known among collectors as Hoadley's upside down movement.

Silas Hoadley retired in 1849 a wealthy man.

ELIAS INGRAHAM (1805 - 1885)

Born in Marlborough, Connecticut, Elias Ingraham served an apprenticeship as a cabinet maker in Hartford and then gained sales experience as a journeyman.

In 1828 he went to Bristol to work under contract for George Mitchell. His task was to design and make wood cases that would successfully compete with the popular bronze looking glass clock case introduced by Chauncey Jerome. Within a few months he designed the carved column and stenciled column shelf clock cases with carved paw feet and was producing them in increasing quantities. They were popular and a large number were made and sold.

In 1830 Ingraham went to work for C. & L. C. Ives under a similar arrangement to that which he had with Mitchell. Here he designed the triple decker shelf case to house eight-day weight driven brass movements. Like his previous venture this one also was a success and during the three years he worked for C. & L. C. Ives, a large number of these cases were made.

Ingraham moved on in 1835 with the intention of working for himself rather than as a contractor for other makers, but during the financial crisis that affected all of America in 1837 heavy business losses were sustained and by 1840 he was bankrupt.

Four years later in 1844 Ingraham entered into a partnership with his brother Andrew and with Elisha Curtis Brewster. Between them they formed the firm Brewster & Ingrahams. During the first year of trading, Elias Ingraham designed the now famous steeple case.

In 1852 the partnership was dissolved and Elias and his brother Andrew continued on their own as E. & A. Ingraham.

In 1855 they suffered a major loss; the factory was almost totally destroyed by fire. The two brothers started another business in Ansonia, Connecticut, but that lasted barely a year and they were back in Bristol.

Elias took his son Edward into partnership in 1857 and they formed the company E. Ingraham & Co. In 1880 the name was changed to The E. Ingraham & Co., and in 1884 it was changed again to The E. Ingraham Co., a name it held until the middle of the twentieth century.

The Doric case was introduced in 1880 and after 1885 the company produced a wide range of shelf clock cases finished in black Japanning. These cases were immensely popular.

Elias Ingraham was the most distinguished American case designer in his time. He entered the business in 1828 and after making his son a partner in 1857 the company was handed down to each succeeding generation.

JOSEPH IVES (1782 - 1862)

Born in Bristol, Connecticut, Joseph Ives was one of the pioneers who developed techniques for the mechanical production of batches of clocks with interchangeable parts. He also injected into the industry new ideas such as roller pinions, wrought brass movements, wagon spring power and tin plate movements.

Ives had the special inborn talents of a mechanical genius and was at the same time a master craftsman. It became apparent, however, that he did not possess the qualities of a good businessman. He concentrated his efforts on ingenuity of design and quality of workmanship and not enough on the marketing of his products. Many times he found himself to be either bankrupt or in serious financial difficulties.

Joseph Ives began his career in his home town in 1811 where he had created a factory in which he made tall case clocks and thirty-hour wood movements with lantern pinions. There is no known documentary evidence to indicate that Ives served any apprenticeship but it is reasonable to assume he must have received some training or instruction.

During those early years he designed a looking glass shelf clock and in 1817 applied for a patent. It was granted, but not until 1822.

Joseph Ives had five brothers, Ira, Amasa Jr., Philo, Shaylor and Chauncey. In 1818 he sold his factory to his youngest brother Chauncey and to Sheldon Lewis. The two partners traded under the name Ives & Lewis and continued the manufacture of Joseph Ives' wood movements and shelf clocks.

After the sale Ives moved into different premises and entered into partnership with two sons of Gideon Roberts, Elias and Titus, and they traded as Joseph Ives & Co.

Within a few months he designed and began production of a new type of eight-day weight driven rack and snail strike movement which he fitted into looking glass shelf clock cases. The movement plates were made of iron and bushed with bronze for the pivot bearings. Iron roller pinions were used to further reduce friction. Both trains of wheels were machined from brass castings. The movement was well designed and well made but far too expensive to be a commercial success. In 1819 the firm of Joseph Ives & Co. went bankrupt and Ives left Bristol.

During the years 1825 - 1830 Ives worked in Brooklyn, Long Island and New York, where he further developed the use of brass. It was here that he invented the wagon spring and used it to provide motive power to an eight-day movement with plates and wheels made of wrought brass. He mounted the wheel arbors between strap plates and thereby economized on the use of raw material. This was America's first brass movement designed to be mass produced by factory methods and as news of his achievments spread, it captured the interest of other makers.

Despite his success the development left Ives heavily in debt, but he was rescued by John Birge, a successful wagon builder operating in Bristol, who offered him a partnership. Ives accepted and in 1830 he returned to Bristol and the firm of Birge & Ives was formed. Birge's interest was that of investment only and Ives was free to continue with his development and manufacture of brass movements.

By this time the supply of wrought brass had become plentiful, so much so that in 1830 the firm of Holmes and Hotchkiss started up in Waterbury, a nearby town, as general suppliers of wrought brass.

In the same year Joseph's brother Chauncey, together with Chauncey's nephew Lawson C. Ives, entered into partnership and started the firm C. & C. L. Ives. Joseph allowed them to produce his wrought brass eight-day movement and they fitted them into a variety of cases designed and made by Elias Ingraham. The firm of C. & C. L. Ives continued until 1836.

In addition to Chauncey and Lawson Ives, permission to manufacture the patented roller pinion was granted to Porteous Ives, the brothers Erastus and Harvey Case and Sylvester Willard who, in 1834, entered into partnership with John Birge and traded as Birge, Case & Co.

Quite suddenly the manufacturers of thirty-hour wood movements were faced with the possibility of losing their markets to these successful producers of brass movements. In desperation, some makers began producing wood movements that ran for eight days but the success of their efforts was very temporary. The additional wheels to the time train needed heavier weights to drive them with the result that broken teeth were all too frequent.

Other makers recognized that the era of wood movements was drawing to an end and to remain in business meant re-equipping their factories for the production of brass movements. To avoid infringement of the roller pinion patent, fixed lantern pinions were invariably used. Two of the principal companies involved were Forestville Manufacturing Co., and E. C. Brewster & Co.

After three years the firm of Birge & Ives was dissolved. Ives continued at Bristol working on his own developing and making brass eight-day movements for others. By this time he had discontinued making strap plates in favor of plates blanked from rolled brass sheet.

In 1839 a number of wealthy residents of Plainville offered Ives financial support if he would go to Plainville and start a clock factory. The offer was accepted and Ives took with him his son Porteous. They purchased a grist mill for conversion and it was from here that they introduced the hour glass clock.

During the years 1839 - 1841 Ives continued producing brass eight-day shelf clocks, in particular those fitted into O. G. cases, but again he put emphasis on development rather than producing low priced clocks in quantity. By 1841 he was in financial difficulty and had to mortgage some of his property.

In 1850 a new company was formed in Bristol trading as Atkins, Whiting & Co. Joseph Ives had an agreement with the partners whereby they were allowed to use his patents and in return he received a percentage of the sales. The use of his wagon spring patent was to be exclusive. Movements sold under their label were thirty-day timepieces with circular plates. To run for thirty days, the force exerted by the wagon spring when wound was considerably more than the screws holding the movement to its case could reasonably be expected to withstand. This was overcome by the use of large cast iron frames made with open decorative plates. The movement was cradled in the top of the frame while the wagon spring was bolted to the bottom of the frame. This arrangement had the effect of becoming a unit independent of the wood clock case.

There were only two types of case in general production; one was a shelf timepiece and the other was a drop octagon wall case.

The company had little financial success and after five years it was closed. Atkins entered into a business arrangement with new partners and the Atkins Clock Manufacturing Co. was formed which replaced the original company. Joseph Ives however did not extend to this new company the authority to use his wagon spring patent and that brought an end to any future use of the patent.

About 1857 Ives introduced the revolutionary tin plate movement with its squirrel cage type rolling pinion crown wheel and the roller verge. These movements were sold to the firms N. L. Brewster and E. Ingraham & Co., who cased and marketed them under their own names.

By this time Joseph Ives had reached the age of seventy-five years. He died five years later, not a wealthy man, but a man who had made considerable advances in the technology of clock design and manufacturing methods.

JOSEPH SHAYLOR IVES

A son of Ira Ives and nephew of Joseph Ives, he was born in Bristol in 1811. Trained by his father he was subsequently employed by Elisha Curtis Brewster from 1832 to 1838.

In 1836 J. S. Ives invented the brass coil spring and sold his idea to E. C. Brewster who used the invention in his clocks for several years.

CHAUNCEY JEROME (1793 - 1868)

During the second quarter of the nineteenth century Chauncey

Jerome was one of America's principal clockmakers. By 1850 his factories were producing more clocks than any other America company but five years later, from mismanagement not entirely of his own making, he was bankrupt.

Jerome was a highly skilled cabinetmaker and a most successful clock case designer, but his greatest ability lay in the promotion of sales. It was he who opened the way for the export of clocks and promoted clock sales in the southern states.

After leaving school, Jerome was trained as a cabinetmaker and carpenter. In 1816 he was working for Eli Terry who had been making experimental pillar and scroll cases by hand but was then preparing to manufacture them in quantity with the help of machinery. Much of the erection was carried out by Jerome under Terry's supervision. Jerome later wrote that he helped to install the first circular saw in Plymouth and that it was he who made the first of Terry's pillar and scroll cases.

About 1819 Jerome started his own business making cases for shelf clocks. Some of them he exchanged for movements which enabled him to sell complete clocks.

In 1821 Jerome sold his business to Terry and moved to Bristol. There he purchased land and a house from George Mitchell and an agreement was reached whereby Jerome was to make payment to Mitchell with a total of three hundred Terry patent movements in three consignments spread over one year.

In 1822 Jerome erected a small workshop on his land and using the experience gained when working for Terry, he installed a circular saw, the first in Bristol. The following year Jerome went to see Chauncey Boardman, a Bristol maker and supplier to the trade of tall case movements and arranged that Boardman would supply him with movements embodying design changes made by Jerome. This was agreed and Boardman supplied Jerome with thirty-hour hang-up movements with winding drums that were reduced in diameter. This modification lessened the distance through which the weight had to fall and allowed Jerome to fit them into cases about four feet tall. The cases were made of stained and varnished pine with a scroll top and reeded side columns. They have been referred to as Connecticut grandmother clocks.

Chauncey Jerome had a younger brother, Noble, who had served an apprenticeship as a movement maker in Plymouth. In 1823 Noble went to Bristol to join his brother. Later that year two Plymouth joiners arrived in Bristol, they were Elijah Darrow and Chauncey Mathews. Chauncey Jerome came to an arrangement with these two men. He sold them his property and they made cases for him under the firm name Darrow & Mathews. Jerome then purchased a workshop close to the river bank.

Darrow & Mathews continued supplying Jerome with movements until, in 1827, they were dissolved. Chauncey and Noble Jerome took Elijah Darrow as a partner and the firm Jeromes & Darrow was formed. That same year Chauncey Jerome introduced his bronze looking glass shelf clock case fitted with a weight driven thirty-hour wood movement designed by his brother Noble. The following year he stopped fitting Noble's movement and instead fitted a movement identical to Terry's patent five wheel train movement but with a thirty-two teeth escape wheel instead of Terry's forty-two teeth. The result was an extremely popular clock and considerable quantities were made.

In 1829 Chauncey Jerome took on his young nephew, Hiram Camp, who was then eighteen years of age.

Other shelf clocks produced by Jeromes & Darrow were looking glass cases with carved columns and splats and with stenciled columns and splats, both types available with thirty-hour or eight-day movements and with short or long pendulums. The eight-day movements were first used about 1831.

The firm also made cornice and column cases, a few pillar and scroll clocks and some Empire style cases with gilt columns. They introduced brass bushes into the plates of thirty-hour wood movements in 1832. Many of their clocks and movements were sold to the trade and never appeared with their name printed on the clock paper.

In 1833 Jeromes & Darrow partnership was dissolved and Chauncey and his brother carried on alone under the name C. & N. Jerome. The new firm obtained brass movements from other makers, probably Joseph Ives or E. C. Brewster.

During the first half of the nineteenth century direct selling to wholesalers and merchants was not enough to expand the clock industry in the north. To increase their distribution, makers had to engage the services of peddlers. These men traveled great distances, many of them deep into the southern states. This intrusion caused many traders in the south to express their disapproval and in 1830 in the state of Tennessee a law was passed making it necessary for all Yankee clock peddlers from the north to pay an annual fee before being allowed to sell in the south. No such licence was needed by those makers who were producing clocks within the southern states.

In 1835 Chauncey and Noble Jerome started a factory in Richmond, Virginia. Movements and cases were made at the Bristol factory and then transported to Richmond where they were assembled and sold as complete clocks under the name C. & N. Jerome without licence and within the law. The assembly factory was subsequently moved to Hamburg, South Carolina.

Then came the business recession of 1837 and the sale of clocks dropped dramatically. Many small companies were forced out of business. Chauncey Jerome decided he must concentrate on the production of low priced reliable clocks and so he put his brother Noble to work developing a cheap one-day brass movement while he designed a small inexpensive case.

The following year Noble introduced a low priced thirty-hour brass movement with an ingenious friction driven strike mechanism that was cheap to produce. Chauncey fitted the movement into a small plain O. G. case and the response was immediate. Everyone wanted a cheap Jerome one-day brass clock and other makers were quick to copy. The demand was so great that in 1839 a new firm, Jeromes, Gilbert, Grant & Co., was formed specifically to deal with sales of the one-day brass O. G. shelf clock. It was a commercial success and in 1840 Chauncey bought out his brother and the other two partners.

In 1842 Jerome astonished other makers when he shipped a consignment of his one-day clocks to England accompanied by his son and a Bristol salesman, Epaphroditus Peck. The clocks were invoiced at one dollar and fifty cents each, and on their arrival in the seaport of Liverpool the customs officials took possession of the consignment. In their opinion, the valuation was too low, resulting in loss of import duty of twenty percent. The British government raised the value by ten percent and paid the invoice. Jerome was so delighted he sent a second shipment and the same thing happened. When the third consignment arrived at Liverpool the officials came to the conclusion that Jerome's invoice valuation was genuine and so the consignment was allowed through. Those clocks were sold in England for about twenty dollars each.

Encouraged by this success Jerome built an export factory in the sea town of New Haven. Here he made clock cases and fitted movements made in his Bristol factories. The completed clocks were then boxed and shipped abroad.

In 1845 Jerome suffered a major loss, one of his Bristol factories was destroyed by fire and very little of value was saved.

During the following ten years, Jerome's exports to England grew steadily and by 1850 he was shipping thirty-hour and eight-day striking clocks in O. G. cases, eight-day striking spring driven beehive and steeple clocks, Empire style cases with spring driven eight-day movements, thirty-hour and eight-day striking clocks in papier maché cases, English style bracket timepieces with spring driven balance wheel lever movements and round and octagonal eight-day striking clocks and timepieces for wall mounting. The movements were stamped:

CHAUNCEY JEROME
New Haven, Conn
U. S. A.

and clock papers were printed

Chauncey Jerome
Manufacturer of
Eight and One Day
BRASS CLOCKS
Time Pieces and Marine Levers
New Haven, Conn
AMERICA

The Jerome Manufacturing Company was later formed at New Haven in 1850.

In 1853 the New Haven Clock Company was incorporated with Hiram Camp as president. This company supplied Jerome with low priced brass movements.

In 1855 Chauncey Jerome had the misfortune of becoming financially involved with one Theodore Terry who had himself lost a clock business through fire in the previous year and was left owing money. A merger took place and Jerome Manufacturing Co. assumed resposibility for the financial obligations. These proved to be far greater than Jerome had been given to understand. That same year at the age of sixty two and after an outstanding sales career he became bankrupt and his business was sold to the New Haven Clock Co.

This was the unhappy ending to a life of successful sales promotion schemes. In former years he had employed hundreds of people in his factories, he was now to become an employee himself. From 1856 to 1857 he worked for Benedict & Burnham in Waterbury making clock cases and from 1857 - 1859 he worked in Ansonia.

In 1859 he was employed by the U. S. Clock Manufacturing Co. in New Haven and went with the company when they moved to Illinois in 1866.

Chauncey Jerome finally returned to New Haven where he died in 1868.

ELI TERRY (1772 - 1852)

Eli Terry was born in East Windsor, Connecticut and apprenticed to Daniel Burnap in East Windsor. He was trained to make wood and brass movements using only hand tools and hand and foot operated machines. He completed his apprenticeship in 1793 and moved to Northbury (Plymouth) where he started his own business making wood and brass movements for tall case clocks. He also invented an equation clock and was granted a patent in 1797. That same year he took on an apprentice named Heman Clark.

By this time Terry had come to realize that there was no future in handmade cases and movements. They took too long to make and were too costly. The demand for clocks was increasing and Terry had the idea of making them by powered machines.

In 1800 he moved into small premises close to flowing water

and installed hand and treadle operated wood-cutting machines. These he converted to power operated by introducing a simple system of shafts, pulleys and belts which were driven by a water wheel. The experiment was a success and he proved to himself that interchangeable components could be produced in batches at a fraction of the cost than when handmade by traditional methods.

At the completion of his apprenticeship Heman Clark remained with Terry and in 1805 they entered into a partnership.

In 1806 Terry purchased a grist mill, probably with ideas of expansion. News of Terry and his factory soon spread and in 1807 he was approached by two brothers, Edward and Levi Porter, with a proposition to manufacture four thousand thirty-hour wood movements in three years. The movements were to be supplied complete with seconds pendulum, dial and hands. The brothers intended reselling them as cased or uncased movements.

Terry agreed to the proposition and a contract was drawn up. He sold his business to Heman Clark and concentrated his efforts on his recent acquisition of the grist mill. He employed two wood joiners, Silas Hoadley and Seth Thomas and with their help set about equipping the mill as a factory. Machines were bought and installed, belt and pulley shafts were put in position, jigs and machine tools were made and raw material was purchased and stored ready for use. One can almost imagine the feelings that Terry must have felt during those months of preparation. He had accepted a challenge that any other clockmaker would have considered as an impossible task.

At the end of the first year he had produced nothing, the full twelve months had been spent in preparing his production and assembly lines. With the arrival of the second year the factory went into production. Many changes were made and all the time the rate of production rose until by the end of that year Terry and his team had produced one thousand movements. By this time their problems and inadequacies had been overcome and in 1810, their third and final year, they completed the contract. The venture had been a complete success. The cost of producing one movement was lower than had ever been achieved by anyone and Eli Terry had laid the foundation for what was to become a thriving international industry.

In the meantime Eli Terry had been giving considerable thought to the idea of producing a striking clock with a thirty-hour movement that would sell at fifteen dollars. In 1810 he sold his business to Hoadley and Thomas and retired to a small workshop at Plymouth Hollow, Connecticut, to explore the feasibility of his idea. He drew up plans and made prototypes and eventually produced the box case clock.

In 1812 Terry bought another water mill and converted it into a clock factory. By continually making improvements to his machining and assembly methods he increased his output to a point where he needed an additional labor force. In 1818 Samuel Terry, a brother of Eli, left his home in East Windsor and brought his sons to Plymouth where he started his own business assembling movements for Eli.

In the meantime Eli Terry had been working on the design of his clock case and in 1819 the first of his pillar and scroll clocks was introduced. Its success was immediate and other makers were quick to copy.

Terry continued to develop his movements but at the same time began to plan for the future of his sons. In 1823 he took Eli Jr. and Henry into the business and traded as Eli Terry & Sons. During the following two years he bought more local property and subsequently controlled three factories under the individual management of Henry, Eli Jr. and Samuel.

During 1824 the two brothers, Eli Sr. and Samuel, entered into partnership and traded as Eli & Samuel Terry. The partnership lasted until 1827 after which Samuel continued on his own for two years and then left Plymouth for Bristol.

Eli's youngest son, Silas, became of age in 1828 and he too joined the firm of Eli Terry & Sons.

Despite the tremendous success he had achieved with his mass produced thirty-hour wood movements he felt that one day the situation would change. It came as no surprise to him when, in 1828 in Brooklyn, a wrought brass movement was introduced by Joseph Ives. Terry recognized the seriousness of the threat to his business and realized he had to do the same. Development would take too long and so, to give himself the time he needed, he and his sons quickly produced a six-train eight-day wood movement, sales of which helped considerably towards maintaining a full order book. By 1832 they had completed their development and production of brass movements began. The following year the firm of Eli Terry & Sons was dissolved.

It would appear that Terry's action was correct because during the years that followed the supply of brass became progressively more plentiful until by 1840 the demand for wood movements evaporated.

In 1852 Eli Terry died. Since then much has been written about him. Many horological historians have referred to him as the father of America's clock manufacturing industry and not without good reason.

SETH THOMAS (1785 - 1859)

Seth Thomas was born in Wolcott, Connecticut. He was far from being a scholar and when his limited schooling was at an end he was trained as a joiner. Thomas's clockmaking career began in 1807 when Eli Terry offered him a job as a wood craftsman, along with Silas Hoadley, working on the Porter contract.

The contract was completed in 1810 after which Terry sold his factory to the two men who carried on manufacturing wood movements under the name Thomas & Hoadley.

Three years later in 1813 Thomas sold out to Hoadley and formed a business of his own. He purchased a clock factory in Plymouth Hollow that had been built four years previously by Heman Clark and continued manufacturing wood movements for tall case clocks.

Two years passed during which there was a noticeable decline in the demand for hang-up and tall case clocks. Eli Terry had introduced his box type case shelf clock which was portable and much less expensive, and Seth Thomas decided to follow his example.

Terry supplied Thomas with thirty-hour, four-wheel train, rack and snail strap movements. Thomas cased them in box type shelf cases and sold them under his own name as Terry patent clocks.

In 1818 or possibly 1819 after Terry had introduced his first pillar and scroll clock, Thomas began converting his own box type cases into pillar and scroll and fitting Terry's four-wheel train strap movements. In 1822 Terry gave Thomas permission to make these movements under licence but with count wheel strike mechanism. This situation continued until about 1824 and then Thomas started fitting Terry's five-wheel train movements to pillar and scroll cases.

Thomas's business prospered and he was fast becoming a rich man. In 1830 he turned his factory over to the manufacture of bronze looking glass clocks with wood movements. The following year he produced a few eight-day wood movements but they were expensive and required very heavy weights.

Eli Terry began producing brass movements in 1832 but Seth Thomas was reluctant to make the change. He continued making thirty-hour wood movements for a few more years but eventually it became obvious that the popularity of wood movements was declining rapidly. In 1838 he began reorganizing his factory for the manufacture of thirty-hour brass weight driven movements. It was a success and by 1850 his annual production was twenty-four thousand valued at sixty thousand dollars and ten years later the annual output was forty thousand with a value of one hundred and twenty thousand dollars. The front plates of his earlier movements were stamped S. Thomas, Plymouth, Conn. U. S. A. while the later movements were stamped Seth Thomas, Thomaston, Conn.

By 1848 steel coil springs had become generally available and the demand for weight driven clocks was noticeably less. In about 1850 Seth Thomas began fitting springs to his movements. He afterwards made very few movements powered by weights.

To keep himself supplied with raw material, Thomas built a brass-rolling mill in 1853 and formed a new firm, Thomas Manufacturing Company. In the same year he organized his clockmaking business into a company naming it Seth Thomas Clock Company. He transferred some of his property to the new company by deed and retained himself as president and principal shareholder. He was sixty-eight years of age and a very rich man when the new company was incorporated. Six years later he died.

Thomas's three sons, Seth Jr., Aaron and Edward successfully carried on the business which continued to expand. In 1862 they introduced eight-day calendar clocks and in 1875 they made calendar clocks primarily for Southern Calendar Clock Company under the trademark Fashion.

Seth Thomas Sons & Company was another new firm. It was formed in 1865 for the specific purpose of manufacturing marine, or lever movements, regulated by a spring balance wheel. A year or two later the company started manufacturing top grade, eighteen-day, pendulum movements to compete with the superbly made imported movements from France but, despite the excellence of workmanship produced by the Seth Thomas Company, the French craftsmanship remained superior.

In 1866, in recognition of the contribution that Seth Thomas made to Plymouth Hollow, the citizens renamed the town Thomaston. It was made official ten years later.

In 1869 the brass mill was sold for the sum of four-hundred-thousand dollars, and in 1872 Seth Thomas Clock Company took over A. S. Hotchkiss & Co., a New York tower clock manufacturer.

Seth Thomas Sons & Co. were successful with their balance wheel movements and about 1875 they began fitting these movements to small round alarm clocks. The demand was almost instantaneous and large quantities were made. In 1879 the Company was incorporated into Seth Thomas Clock Company. The total number of employees of the firm exceeded eight hundred. The same year they introduced a range of finely made regulators in a variety of styles and each was fitted with a precision mercury pendulum.

The last major event that took place during the nineteenth century within Seth Thomas Clock Company was in 1882 when they started a production line for the manufacture of jeweled pocket watches.

When Seth Thomas died he was succeeded by his son Seth Jr., and in turn by his grandson and then his great grandson, both their names being Seth. The company finally left the family in 1932 when it became part of General Time Instruments Corporation. The great grandson died the following year.

THE WILLARDS

Benjamin Willard Sr. and his wife Sarah lived in Grafton, Massachusetts where they brought up a family of twelve children.

Below is part of the family tree showing only those members connected with the making of clocks and watches, excluding Benjamin Sr. and his wife.

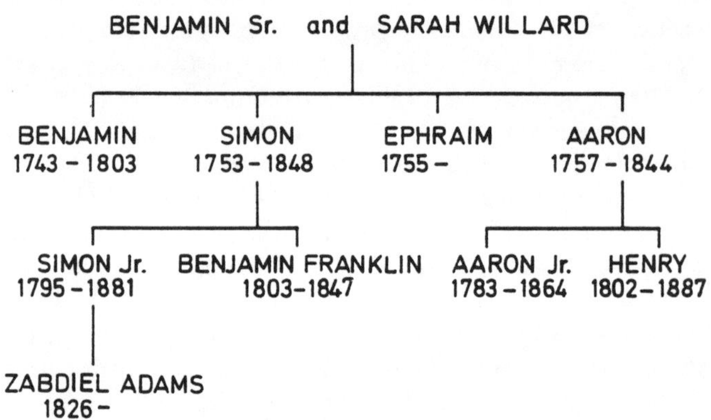

BENJAMIN

Very little is known about Benjamin, the first of the Willard clockmakers. In 1764 he bought some property from his father and set himself up in a clockmaking business. About 1771 he moved to Roxbury and continued his clockmaking activities which seem to have been confined to tall case clocks. Some good examples are known, mostly with elegant brass dials, probably imported from England.

SIMON

Simon was an indifferent scholar with little or no interest for learning anything academic. At a very early age it became obvious that his interest was in mechanical things, so much so that an English clockmaker accepted him as an apprentice when he was only twelve years old. His rate of learning and his ability to acquire hand skills was quite extraordinary. Little more than a year after his apprenticeship began, he was making a striking tall case clock without the aid of machinery. Both movement and case were made entirely by hand. It is reasonable to assume that at the completion of his apprenticeship he went into business on his own because clocks are known which carry the inscription Simon Willard, Grafton.

Some time later, probably about 1778, he moved to Roxbury where he set up a workshop and continued to produce handmade, tall case clocks and Massachusetts shelf clocks until the turn of the century.

In 1801 he introduced his Improved Timepiece, later known as the banjo, for which the demand was so great that he gave up making tall case clocks. Simon was granted a patent for his timepiece, but for some obscure reason he appears to have made no attempt to stop other makers from copying his design. Had he done so, or had he allowed manufacture to take place under a licence, he would most certainly have benefited from his ideas. As it was, others lined their purses at his expense while he remained relatively poor.

Simon was never good at business; it seems he concentrated on quality of material and standard of workmanship; only the best was good enough, and cost seems to have been of secondary importance. This was particularly so with his turret clocks and clocks for public buildings and government offices. In 1831, at the age of seventy-eight, he made a turret clock for the Old State House, Boston, and six years later he installed two clocks, commissioned by the government in Washington D. C. One clock can be seen in the Supreme Court and the other in Statuary Hall fitted into Franzoni's famous sculpture of Clio.

Simon made two large fine gallery clocks with gilded cases surmounted by a gilded eagle. One was installed in the First Church of Roxbury and the other in the Second Church of Dorchester. He was also responsible for the clocks at Harvard College.

Simon remained at his Roxbury workshop until he retired in 1839. His range of clocks included tall case, Massachusetts shelf, banjo, gallery, turret, banjo type regulators and wall regulators.

As far as is known, all his movements were handmade and of brass.

EPHRAIM

Like his brother Benjamin, little is known of Ephraim's activities. It is possible that he received his training as a clockmaker from Benjamin. A few tall case clocks by him are known. He began his working life at Grafton and then moved on to Roxbury in 1798, Boston in 1801 and New York City in 1805.

AARON

There is no documented evidence showing to whom Aaron was apprenticed, if indeed he was. It therefore seems reasonable to assume that he received some form of training from his brothers, even though Simon was only four years his senior.

He must have been in business at his birthplace because clocks are known bearing the signature Aaron Willard, Grafton.

In 1780 Aaron moved to Roxbury and operated a clock workshop not far from his brother Simon. It was here that he grew to realize that success could never be achieved by making individual clocks by hand.

With this in mind he moved to Boston some time during the 1790's and started what quickly became a large factory. Here he made tall case clocks, wall clocks, Massachusetts shelf clocks, gallery clocks, banjo timepieces and regulators. At first the Massachusetts shelf clocks were produced in a variety of styles in great quantities and then the banjo timepieces took over and they became the principal product.

Aaron soon began to prosper, and other men sensing the atmosphere of success settled down in the district and formed a community that included dial painters, cabinet makers, machinists, movement makers, founders and lead molders. Apart from these specialists Aaron had full-time employees engaged in the production of clocks. By 1823 his business was so successful that he was able to retire a very rich man. The running of the business was handed over to his son, Aaron Jr.

AARON JR.

Aaron Jr. was born in Roxbury and became apprenticed to his father. In about 1823, when his father retired, he took control of the clock factory and carried on the business, making very few changes. He continued making the same range of clocks as his father, turning out banjo timepieces in great quantities, usually with ornamental base pieces. It was Aaron Jr. who introduced the lyre clock, and these he made in a wide variety of styles and in large numbers. He also conducted an extensive repair shop.

Aaron Jr became a very wealthy man and, like his father, he decided to retire early. He had two children, a boy and a girl. The boy died at an early age and the girl died before her father. There was therefore no one to whom the business could be left, and so Aaron Jr. decided to close down.

SIMON JR.

Simon was born in Roxbury. His was not a happy childhood; he had to work hard and it was not until he was ten years of age that he received any regular education. When he was eighteen he enlisted at West Point as an army cadet, but after three years he resigned his commission and returned to Roxbury. He then applied himself to the crockery business, without success, and after eight years he had to give it up.

Simon Jr. then joined his father and studied clockmaking, but two years later he left and went to New York City where he studied the manufacture of chronometers and pocket watches. His ability to learn and understand such a complex subject must have been quite outstanding because two years later, in 1828, he returned intending to start his own business in Boston.

Simon Jr. had no money and with such little training his father condemned the idea as absurd. Nevertheless Simon Jr. opened a store and advertised in the press "......CHRONOMETERS, Duplex Virgule, Lepine, Horizontal Repeating, and Patent Lever watches repaired; also Chimney and Musical Clocks......".

Such was Simon Jr.'s skill that in 1832 he made a beautiful astronomical regulator. The movement was a precision instrument of such high standard of accuracy that it was used as the master timepiece by all railroads in New England.

The business was a success and it flourished. Boston Harbor was a busy port. Sea captains took their chronometers to Simon Jr. for rating and collected then when their ships were ready to sail away. His watch repair business grew and he advertised by inserting into the back of the case a circular watch paper that was printed:

SIMON WILLARD JR.
9
Congress Street
BOSTON
CHRONOMETERS
for ascertaining Longitude
adjusted.
CHIMNEY
& Musical Clocks
repaired

Simon Jr. had a son, Zabdiel Adams, who served an apprenticeship with his father. In 1850 Simon Jr. took his son into partnership, after which he traded under the name Simon Willard & Son.

HENRY

Henry was born in Boston. Close to his home was the workshop of William Fisk, a very skilled cabinetmaker. It was with him that Henry served an apprenticeship specializing in the making of clock cases.

Henry produced very fine work and made many cases for his father, his brother and for his cousin, Simon Jr.

BENJAMIN FRANKLIN

Benjamin Franklin was born in Roxbury and had a similar childhood to that of his brother Simon Jr. He learned clockmaking from his father during which time he demonstrated his inheritance of his father's skills. He made very few clocks, but in 1844 at his brother's shop at 9 Congress St., he made an astronomical clock even finer than that of his brother.

The movement was large. The brass plates were thick and heavy and were held by unusually large pillars. Pivot bearings were jewelled with sapphires and the whole assembly highly polished. The movement was encased in a brass frame with glass panels at back and sides. A large compensating pendulum was used carrying fifty-six pounds of mercury. A device was fitted so that the unusually heavy pendulum could be detached from the movement and lowered onto a support, allowing the movement to be removed.

The polished mahogany case was made by Charles Crane Crehore (1793 - 1879). It was he who made the case for Simon Jr.'s astronomical regulator and who frequently made cases for Simon. The astronomical regulator was a very costly and superb piece of workmanship for which the Massachusetts Charitable Mechanics Association awarded Benjamin Franklin Willard a gold medal.

ZABDIEL ADAMS

Zabdiel, the last of the Willards to be involved in clocks and watches, was born in Roxbury and was later apprenticed to his father in 1841. In 1850 he entered into partnership with his father, and in the space of a few years became widely acknowledged as a leading authority on pocket chronometers. He retired in 1870.

APPENDIX 1

Glossary of Terms

Acanthus - Any prickly leaved plant.

Acid Etching - Etching or frosting a design on glass tablets was a popular form of decoration among wood casemakers, particularly those of steeple clocks. The effect was produced by acid. A clay tablet was employed that had a flat surface into which the design had been recessed. Hot wax was poured over the design, completely filling the recesses and surplus wax was scraped away leaving the original flat surface.

The clay tablet was turned over and placed face down on the glass tablet that was to be etched. When the clay tablet was cold it was removed, the wax remaining on the glass to which it had adhered.

The glass was then turned over and suspended in acid fumes where it remained until sufficient depth of corrosion had taken place.

A more modern method is to use an adhesive paper in place of a wax impression.

Acorn Clock - A shelf clock with a frame of laminated wood to permit bending during manufacture. The upper half is shaped as an acorn and the lower half is similar to a wine decanter.

Alarm - A mechanical device that is manually preset and which causes a hammer to strike rapidly against a bell at a predetermined time. The device can be built into the movement or it can be a separate unit but each is controlled by the time train.

Amplitude - The distance covered by the bob of a pendulum in a normal swing from one side to the other.

Anchor Escapement - This invention is generally attributed to Dr. Robert Hooke but believed to have been used first by William Clement of London about 1671. It requires very little angular movement for efficient operation, less than five degrees in fact, which means that the pendulum is also limited to the small amount of movement. This has the advantage of being able to use a long pendulum with a one-second rating, which gives greatly improved timekeeping, instead of the inferior half-second short bob pendulum.

Apparent Time - See Solar Time.

Arbor - A round iron or steel spindle that carries a pinion, wheel, detent, lever, hammer or anchor. The ends are reduced in diameter to form pivots which are supported in pivot holes drilled in the plates of the movement. The square or radiused collar formed by shaping the pivot serves to locate the arbor between the plates and the reduced diameter lowers the surface friction. The diameters of the arbors and pivots will vary according to the load under which they function.

Arc - The angle, expressed in degrees, through which a pendulum moves in a normal swing from one side to the other.

Automata - A mechanical device which is driven by the strike train or time train and which serves no purpose other than novelty. Examples are a girl in a swing, windmill, sails and a tossing ship.

Back Plate - See Plates

Balance - The energy stored in a wheel train after a clock has been wound is released in small measured amounts under the influence of the swinging motion of a controller. When the controller is a wheel it is known as the balance.

Balance Spring or Hairspring - A volute or flat spiral spring is used to give the balance greater accuracy. The inner end of the spring is attached to the balance staff while the outer end is fixed to a movement plate. When the balance oscillates, first in one direction and then in reverse, so the spring winds and unwinds.

Banjo - The colloquial name for Simon Willard's Patent Improved Timepiece.

Barrel - The container in which a mainspring is coiled.

Beat - The "tic-toc" of a pendulum timekeeper is the sound made by the escape wheel teeth striking the pallets of the escapement at each swing of the pendulum. This is called the beat and the sound should be steady. If the clock is not in beat it will produce a long "tic" and a short "toc" indicating that the timekeeper is not upright or that the pendulum crutch is in need of adjustment. Similarly, the ticking of a balance wheel escapement of a lever or marine movement must be steady or the movement will stop.

Beehive clock - A shelf clock with a curved and pointed top that is classically described as round Gothic because of its similarity to architectural arches of that era. The colloquial name is beehive. It was the first American mass-produced clock to be fitted with coil springs for motive power.

Bezel - The wood or metal ring that holds the dial glass.

Black Mantel - Shelf clocks from about 1875 made of black enameled wood, black marble or black cast iron and usually with the escapement on view in front of the dial.

Bob - The weight on the end of a pendulum. Originally referred to the small round weight which was screwed onto the lower end of a half-seconds pendulum, known as a bob pendulum. Now more generally used when referring to the weight of any pendulum.

Box Case - Eli Terry's prototype mass production shelf case which was the forerunner of the pillar and scroll clock. It was a plain mahogany box shape with no form of decoration.

Box-on-Box - Another name for the Massachusetts shelf clock.

Bracket Clock - In 1658 the first English made spring driven pendulum clock appeared in London and it became known as a bracket clock. Some of the early settlers from England probably introduced them into the American colonies and about 1770 American made cases began to appear. They continued to be made in small quantities until about 1830.

Break Arch - Sometimes called broken arch. Some grandfather and bracket clock dials had an arched top, the diameter of which was less than the width of the dial plate. The tops of the cases were invariably shaped to match and these arches were known as break arch.

Bronze Looking Glass - Introduced by Chauncey Jerome, the case was similar to the pillar and scroll looking glass clock except that the top carried a splat instead of swan neck scrolls and finials and at each side of the door was a wide half-round column. The case was decorated with bronze powder stencils.

Bushing - When pivot holes in movement plates become badly worn the arbors can no longer be located in their correct positions due to the excessive sideways movement of the pivots. This in turn affects the depthing of the wheels and the movement either functions badly or stops. The rate of wear is accelerated by lack of oil and is more pronounced in weight driven clocks. The remedy is to disassemble the movement, enlarge the worn pivot holes by drilling and press in bushings made for the purpose. These bushings are predrilled, and when in position in the plates the holes are enlarged to the size required for the pivot.

Calendar - Some movements are fitted with a calendar mechanism which is driven by the time train. Painted cylinders or discs are caused to rotate behind apertures in the dial, or hands rotate in ancillary dials. Indications are year, month, day of the week, date, moon phase or any combination of them. Manual adjustment is required for months with less than 31 days and for leap years. Such a mechanism is called a simple calendar. A more sophisticated mechanism that is fully automatic and requires no manual adjustment is called perpetual calendar.

Cannon Pinion - Sometimes referred to as the cannon wheel, it belongs to the motion work or dial wheels as they are sometimes called. Part of the cannon pinion is a pipe that is squared at its front end to carry the minute hand. The pipe fits snugly over the center arbor and is driven by it under the influence of a thin friction spring, the resistance of which is overcome by slight pressure when resetting the hands.

Capital - The carved or molded top of an architectural column.

Carved Column and Stenciled Column Clock - Designed by Elias Ingraham in 1828, these shelf clock cases were introduced by George Mitchell to compete with Jerome's bronze looking glass clock. The cases were tall and had a carved splat at the top and a carved or stenciled column at each side of the door.

Case-on-Case - See Massachusetts Shelf Clock

Cast Iron Back Plate - Invented by Charles Kirk in 1843 for use with brass coil springs. Cast integral with the plate were two circular wells that housed the springs. The movement was protected from damage in the event of a spring failure and the springs were prevented from wandering during run down.

Center Seconds - A slender seconds hand pivoting at the center of the dial and reaching the minute divisions. Sometimes referred to as a sweep seconds hand.

Chapter Ring - The circular band on a dial in which the numerals or chapters are engraved or painted.

Chronometer - A timekeeper capable of maintaining exceedingly accurate time. The movement is usually fitted with a detent escapement.

Circa or C - Latin meaning around or about.

Click - See Ratchet

Clock - See Timekeeper.

Compensating Pendulum - With a rise in temperature a pendulum will expand and increase its length, which has the effect of slowing down the movement. With a drop in temperature the reverse takes place. A compensating pendulum is so designed that changes in temperature are automatically compensated and the distance between the center of gravity of the pendulum weight and the center of suspension remains constant.

Complicated Work - Mechanisms that are additional to timekeeping and striking, such as chime, calendar and astronomical.

Count Wheel - See Locking Plate.

Crane Clock - Instead of the conventional swinging pendulum, Aaron Dodd Crane introduced a rotary or torsion pendulum. It consisted of a long ribbon of steel at the lower end of which was a metal ball or group of balls forming the pendulum weight. This group of balls slowly rotated in a horizontal plane until the twisting of the steel brought the weight to a halt and caused it to reverese direction. This type of clock will run for twelve months at one winding and for this reason is known as a year clock. They are not to be confused with the more modern 400-day clocks made in Germany.

Crown Wheel Escapement - See Verge Escapement.

Crutch - This is a length of soft iron wire attached at one end to the anchor arbor while the other end is shaped,usually in the form of a fork or loop, to embrace the pendulum rod closely. With each impulse of the escape wheel against the pallets of the anchor, the crutch is caused to swing taking with it the pendulum. This allows the pendulum to be suspended independently of the escapement. There is no crutch with a verge escapement where the bob pendulum is secured to the end of the verge.

Dead Beat Escapement - Similar in action to the anchor escapement but capable of maintaining more accurate time. There is no recoil.

Detent - An arm acting as a stop or pawl.

Dial Pillar - The pillars in a plate frame movement that hold the dial to the front plate. Each pillar is riveted at one end to the dial plate, while the other end passes through a hole in the front plate and is held by a taper pin passing through the pillar behind the front plate.

Dial Wheels - See Motion Train.

Direct Fusee - See Fusee.

Double Decker - A variation to a shelf clock design giving the impression of two sections standing one upon the other. Particularly applicable to carved column and stenciled column clocks.

Drum - The barrel onto which the gut or cord of a weight driven clock is wound.

Equation Clock - A clock capable of indicating the difference between mean time and solar time.

Equation of Time - The amount of time in minutes and seconds that must be added to or subtracted from solar time to give mean time.

Escapement - See Movement.

Finial - A wood or brass decoration used on the tops of clock cases and frequently taking the form of an acorn, a flaming torch or a pineapple.

Fly - A fan at the end of a strike train which acts as an air brake and slows down the rate of strike.

Front Plate - See Plates.

Full Plate - A movement plate that is not pierced or cut away.

Fusee - A device sometimes fitted to spring driven movements to compensate for a progressive reduction of energy as the spring unwinds. It ensures that a constant torque is applied to the wheel train at all times. The English method is to mount the fusee on the great wheel arbor and is known as a direct fusee. The American method is to carry the fusee on the mainspring arbor when it is known as a reverse fusee.

Gathering Pallet - The piece in a rack and snail strike mechanism that gathers up the rack one tooth for each blow of the hammer.

Gesso - A plaster of Paris surface prepared as a ground for painting.

Gilding - A chemical or electrolytic process of depositing a thin film of gold alloy on a base metal.

Girandole Timepiece - A wall clock designed by Lemuel Curtis about 1814 and which is now freely described as America's most beautiful clock. Not unlike a banjo in general construction.

Gold Leaf - The process of applying extremely thin gold sheet to an adhesive surface of gold size.

Graham Pendulum - A compensating pendulum invented by George Graham in 1726. It consists of a jar of mercury held in a cradle in place of a pendulum weight. When the temperature rises the pendulum rod expands. At the same time, the mercury rises in the jar and compensates for the elongation of the rod.

Grandfather Clock - The colloquial name for tall case clocks, known equally as tall clocks and longcase clocks.

Grandmother Clock - A much shorter version of the grandfather clock.

Great Wheel - The first wheel in a train. In weight driven movements it is mounted on the winding drum and in spring driven movements it is on the mainspring barrel or the fusee, if fitted.

Gridiron Pendulum - A compensating pendulum invented by John Harrison about 1726. It consists of an assembly of brass and steel rods arranged alternately immediately above the pendulum weight. The coefficient of expansion of brass is greater than that of steel and the difference in expansion compensates for the expansion of the pendulum rod.

Groaner Movement - A 30-hour wood movement designed by Chauncey Boardman c.1825 with an overhead strike. The sound made by the meshing of the wheels during striking has earned for itself the name groaner.

Gut Line - See Lines.

Hairspring - See Balance Spring.

Half Clock - See Massachusetts Shelf Clock.

Half Seconds Pendulum - A pendulum that swings from one side to the other in a half-second. Its length is a little over nine and one half inches.

Harrison's Maintaining Spring - When a weight-driven or spring-driven clock is being wound, motive power is removed from the time train and the hands cease to record the passing of time. Any device that supplies temporary power to the time train during winding is known as maintaining power. Such a device was invented by John Harrison in 1726 for use with weight driven movements and is known as Harrison's maintaining spring.

Hollow Column Clock - These are weight driven shelf clocks introduced about 1828 with two large diameter hollow columns, one at each side, in which the weights function. The columns can be made of wood or sheet iron.

Hoop Wheel - One of the wheels in a count wheel strike train. On one face is a hoop the rim of which holds up a detent which action allows the count wheel to rotate.

Hour Glass Clock - Introduced by Joseph Ives about 1841, this shelf clock was made of laminated wood and shaped like an hour glass or egg timer. It was powered by a form of inverted wagon spring screwed to the underside of the case roof.

Inside Outside Escapement - An accepted collector's description of a type of movement fitted by Eli Terry into his pillar and scroll clocks, in which the pendulum and escapement takes up a position immediately behind the dial.

Iron Front Clocks - Shelf Clocks with cases of cast iron.

Japanning - The Japanese art of applying laquer to wood to produce colored designs and pictures for the purpose of decoration.

Kidney Dial - The distinctive and unique shape of the dial opening in the majority of Massachusetts shelf clocks.

Labels - See Papers.

Ladder Movement - This was a spring-driven one-day brass movement pendulum control introduced by Silas Burnham Terry. The movements were fitted to small wood shelf timepieces. The wheels of the train were held in line by plates three quarters of one inch in width which were mounted vertically in the case.

Lantern Pinion - This type of pinion consists of two circular end plates supporting a number of wire pins equally spaced.

Leaves - Pinions that are cut with teeth are said to have leaves. The term teeth is used for wheels only.

Lever or Marine Movement - A spring driven movement that is controlled by a balance wheel escapement.

Lighthouse Clock - A very rare shelf clock by Simon Willard. The dial and movement are covered by a tall glass dome and are mounted on the top of a circular trunk and base. The general effect is that of a lighthouse.

Lines - Weights of early clocks were invariably suspended from stranded wire cable, particularly for the heaviest weights. Cat gut then became more generally used. These two products are still available from material suppliers, but a more modern replacement is braided nylon cord.

Locking Plate - The locking plate or count wheel is a toothed wheel in the locking plate strike mechanism which carries a hoop on one face. In the rim of the hoop are eleven spaces, their distance apart being progressively greater. All the time the wheel rotates the hammer will continue to strike. Control is exercised by arranging for a hooked detent to drop into one of the spaces in which position the wheel is locked and further striking is prevented.

Long Case Clock - See Grandfather Clock.

Looking Glass Clock - This was a tall, weight-driven wall clock introduced in 1817 by Joseph Ives fitted with a full length mirror in its door. Other makers copied the design.

Lunette - The area occupied by the dome-shaped top of the break arch dial.

Lyre - A wall timepiece introduced about 1810 having design features similar to that of the banjo but with a marked resemblance to the lyre musical instrument in the design of the neck.

Mainspring - The coil springs that supply motive power to the time and strike trains in a spring-driven movement.

Maintaining Power - Any mechanical device that supplies an auxiliary driving force to the time train during the winding operation. See Harrison's maintaining spring.

Marine Movement - See Lever Movement.

Marquetry - Cabinet work inlaid with pieces of different colored woods to produce a variety of patterns and designs both geometric and pictorial.

Massachusetts Shelf Clock - Introduced about 1760 by Simon Willard. Probably the first American shelf clock. Sometimes referred to as half clock,case-on-case, or box-on-box. Their cases include some design features which traditionally belong to grandfather clocks. Many have the appearance of a clock standing on a separate cabinet.

Mean Time - The result of dividing the solar year into equal periods of time. All general use clocks indicate mean time.

Meridian - When the path of the sun reaches its highest point.

Mock Pendulum - Sometimes called false pendulum. It is a miniature pendulum positioned close behind a curved slot in the dial and kept in motion by the clock pendulum. It serves as a visual indication that the movement is functioning and was frequently fitted to bracket clocks.

Moon Dial - A popular subsidiary dial fitted in the break arch of a grandfather clock dial. A slowly rotating disc behind an aperture in the dial plate indicated the age and phase of the moon.

Motion Train - The wheels and pinions behind the dial that carry the hands. Sometimes referred to as dial wheels.

Motive Power - See Movement.

Movement - A simple mechanical timepiece consists of a train of wheels for driving the hands with a source of power at one end and a controlling device at the other end. In America the wheels that drive the hands are referred to as the time train; in Great Britain the term going train is used. The source of power, known as the motive power, is a hanging weight or coiled spring that transfers its energy to the wheel train through a ratchet. At the other end of the train is an escapement that prevents the wheels from rotating at high speed by placing an obstruction in the path of the last wheel. This wheel, which is called the escape wheel, is released one tooth at a time and so all wheels are allowed to rotate in a series of small measured distances. Similarly, strike and chime mechanisms have their own wheel trains and their own independent sources of motive power, but they rely on the time train to set them in motion.

O. G. Case - A wood clock case rather like a heavy picture frame made from ogee section. This was the style used by Chauncey Jerome for his one-day brass movement clocks that he shipped to England in 1842 and which marked the beginning of America's export trade of clocks.

Ogee - A molding S-shaped in section.

Oil Sink - A countersunk machining around a pivot hole in the outside face of a movement plate in which oil is retained.

One-Seconds Pendulum - A pendulum that swings from one side to the other in one second.

Outside Escapement - A term used by collectors to describe a particular design of movement used by Eli Terry in his experimental pillar and scroll clocks. The escape wheel, anchor, crutch and upper half of the pendulum were visible in front of the dial.

Pallet - The faces of an anchor, in an anchor escapement, that alternately lock and release the escape wheel teeth.

Papers - Clock papers, or labels as they are frequently called, were first printed about 1800. They were pasted to the inside face of the back of the case. Early papers announced the name of the maker and place of origin, but it was not long before makers added small announcements to the public assuring them of the reliability of the clock they had purchased. As time passed, clock papers became more elaborate until, by 1820, papers included full setting up instructions and detailed directions for winding and resetting hands. These papers play an important part in closely identifying a clock.

Parcel-Gilt - Partially gilded.

Patent Timepiece - The name given by Simon Willard to his banjo timepiece and which appeared on his patent documents.

Pendulum - A weight suspended from a fixed point and which is free to swing without obstruction. In a clock the action of the swinging weight is used to regulate the speed of the movement.

Pendulum Bob - See Bob.

Pilaster - Originally an architectural term. It means a square column partly built into a wall.

Pillar and Scroll - A shelf clock introduced by Eli Terry in 1818 and subsequently produced by other makers throughout the century. There were many experimental clocks, but the final was introduced in 1822 and it became America's first mass-produced shelf clock.

Pillar and Scroll Looking Glass - A variation of Terry's pillar and scroll clock with a looking glass in the lower portion of the door. Introduced by the firm Ives & Lewis.

Pinion - A toothed wheel with less than twenty teeth usually driven by a train wheel. The teeth of a pinion are called leaves. Originally they were filed to shape but early in the eighteenth century English clockmakers discovered that if iron wire was pulled through a steel drawer plate with a hole shaped to the profile of the pinion, the wire was transformed into a continuous pinion that could be cut to any desired length. This was known as pinion wire. See Lantern Pinion.

Pivot - The reduced diameter at the ends of an arbor that are supported in pivot holes drilled in movement plates.

Plates - The two plates of a movement are known as the back plate and the front plate. That which is closer to the dial is the front plate, the other is the back plate.

Rack - A lever in the rack and snail strike mechanism that is centrally pivoted. One end carries a pin that is in contact with the cam-shaped rim of a snail. The angle of the rack will determine how many teeth are exposed to the gathering pallet and consequently how many hammer blows will be made.

Rack and Snail Strike - This method of strike control superceded the locking plate or count wheel method. It is linked to the hour hand and cannot become out of sequence with the time train. It will always strike the hour indicated by the hour hand.

Ratchet - When a movement is in need of winding it becomes necessary to break into the chain of moving parts so that one of them can be turned in reverse to wind up the weight or spring. This facility is provided by fitting a ratchet to the great or main wheel. A ratchet comprises a spring-loaded click that engages with a set of teeth. When turned in the direction of winding, the click rides the teeth against the tension of the click spring but when winding stops, the click engages the teeth and transmits the motive power to the train of wheels.

Rate - A movement is said to have a good rating when it maintains steady timekeeping. Even when a movement has a gain or loss it is still said to have a good rate providing the gain or loss is steady and never varies. Such a movement will maintain accurate timekeeping by adjusting the rating nut beneath the pendulum weight or by moving the regulator in the case of a spring balance movement.

Recoil - The momentary backward rotation of the escape wheel of recoil escapements. This can be seen by observing the small seconds hand of a grandfather clock, the hand being carried on the pipe of the escape wheel.

Recoil Escapement - The most usual form of recoil escapement is the anchor escapement.

Regulator - Usually a wall-hung timekeeper with a long pendulum and without strike mechanism or any form of complicated work. The movement is accurate, and it is fitted with a dead-beat escapement and a compensating pendulum.

It is a precision timepiece without refinements and was not intended for domestic use. They are frequently to be found in the workshops of clock repairers who use them as standards where precise time is a requirement.

Reverse Fusee - See Fusee.

Reverse Painting - The fronts of many clocks were decorated with oil paintings but to prevent the paintings from being damaged they were painted on the inside face of glass panels or tablets as they are known. The art was in applying the colors in the reverse order; the last color had to be applied first.

Ripple Molding - An applied wood molding with a ripple surface obtained by first steaming the wood and then subjecting it to a press with a ripple impression. These moldings were frequently used on steeple clock cases and beehive cases.

Roller Pinion - Invented by Joseph Ives in 1832, it was a lantern pinion with rollers instead of wires. This arrangement greatly reduced friction.

Rotary Pendulum - See Crane Clock.

Seat Board - The wood platform on which the movement of a tall case clock stands.

Seconds Pendulum - See One-Seconds Pendulum.

Snail - A disc in the rack and snail strike mechanism with a stepped rim against which one end of the rack lever comes to rest after being released. This new position of the rack lever controls the number of hammer blows to be made.

Solar Time - The time indicated on a sundial according to the position of the sun in the sky. Sometimes referred to as apparent or true time. A solar day commences when the sun leaves the meridian and ends when the sun returns to the same position, but the time taken to complete the cycle is different each day.

Spandrel - The space between the curve of a chapter ring and the corner of a square dial plate.

Splat - A decorative wood panel on top of a case. Frequently carved or bronzed.

Spring Barrel - See Barrel.

Steeple - A shelf clock designed by Elias Ingraham in 1844. The classical name is sharp Gothic. The top of the case is gabled and at each side of the door is a spire or steeple.

Stenciling - To paint by brushing over a perforated plate.

Strap Plate or Frame - A wood or brass movement with plates made from strips riveted or screwed together to form an open plate.

Suspension Spring - The spring by which a pendulum is suspended.

Sweep Seconds Hand - See Center Seconds.

Tall Case Clock - See Grandfather Clock.

Tall Clock - See Grandfather Clock.

Timby Solar Timepiece - A shelf timepiece with a rotating globe of the world supposedly to enable both solar time and mean time to be read and to show the difference in time between any two points on the globe.

Timekeeper - A term that includes timepieces and clocks. A timepiece has a time train only, while a clock has time and strike trains. It is common practice, however, to refer to them both as clocks.

Tin Plate Movement - Introduced in 1859 by Joseph Ives, the wheels and circular plates were made of thick tinned iron sheet ribbed for added strength. Pivots ran in brass bushings and roller pinions were used.

Torrington Movement - To avoid infringement of Eli Terry's patent covering his 30-hour wood movement a group of clockmakers in Torrington developed a wood movement with plates that took up the full width of pillar and scroll cases but were quite narrow.

Torsion Pendulum - See Crane Clock.

Train - A line of wheels and pinions of calculated gear ratio so arranged that they transmit motive power fron one to the other terminating at the escapement.

Transition Clock - A shelf clock that appeared about 1830. The design of the case resembled the pillar and scroll in some respects but other design features subsequently appeared in the stenciled and carved column clock cases.

True Time - See Solar Time.

Verge Escapement - Sometimes known as a crown wheel escapement, it is the oldest form of clock escapement. It was used in conjunction with a foliot balance on the earliest known, weight-driven public clocks and was still being used in some clocks up to the late nineteenth century.

Wagon Spring - An early form of spring power introduced before coil springs became commercially available. It resembled a wagon leaf spring and was bolted to the bottom of the case. From each end of the spring a chain was led away to a drum, and when the chains were wound around the drums the ends of the spring were lifted and the spring tension was increased.

Wag-on-Wall Clock - A tall case clock movement complete with dial, hands and weights that was hung on a wall, eliminating the expense of a case.

Warning - A few minutes before the clock is due to strike the strike train is released to enable it to perform its preliminary motions. The train is then stopped by the warning piece and held until exactly on the hour. Immediately the strike train is released; for the second time, the pin wheel actuates the hammer tail, and striking begins.

Weights - These are usually made of iron, lead or brass in a variety of shapes or sizes dependent on the type of movement and design of case. In practical terms the poundage of a weight needs to be a few ounces more than is required to drive the movement when it is clean, unworn and oiled.

Wheel Count - To calculate the number of swings made by a pendulum in one hour, multiply together the number of teeth in each wheel of the time train and divide by the result of multiplying together the number of leaves in each pinion. The number of teeth in the escape wheel must be doubled because each tooth acts on both pallets separately and is equivalent to two beats of the pendulum.

Year Clock - See Crane Clock.

APPENDIX 2

Dates of Interest

c 1685	Tall case clocks imported. They came from England.
c 1695	Grandfather clocks first produced in Pennsylvania.
c 1705	Arrival of first watch and clock makers in the colonies.
c 1745	Wood movements first made. Probably by Benjamin Cheyney Jr.
c 1760	Simon Willard introduced Massachusetts shelf clocks.
c 1770	Dwarf tall case clocks appeared.
c 1770	Bracket clocks first made in America.
1775-1783	The War of American Independence (The American Revolution).
c 1792	Paper dials introduced.
c 1800	First clock papers printed.
1802	Simon Willard granted patent for Improved Timepiece (banjo).
1810	Eli Terry introduced mass production of wood movements. Brought to an end the system of apprenticeship.
1812-1814	War between the United States and Great Britain.
1814	Eli Terry introduced box case clocks with strap plate movements.

c 1814	Lemuel Curtis developed the girandole clock.
1817	Joseph Ives introduced the looking glass clock.
1818	Eli Terry introduced the pillar and scroll clock.
c 1821	Simon Willard introduced the lighthouse clock.
1822	Eli Terry introduced his final model of pillar and scroll, which became America's first mass production shelf clock.
1825	Joseph Ives introduced the wagon spring.
c 1825	Clock hands ceased to be cut and shaped by hand. They were stamped from thin sheet metal.
1827	Chauncey Jerome introduced bronze looking glass clocks.
c 1829	Elias Ingraham designed carved and stenciled column cases.
c 1830	Transition clock appeared.
1830	Elias Ingraham designed double-deck carved and stenciled column cases.
1830	Joseph Ives introduced the first brass movement capable of being mass produced.
1831	Elias Ingraham designed triple deck case for carved column clocks.
1833	Joseph Ives granted patent for roller pinions.
1835	Steel wire bell (cathedral gong) introduced by James Breckenbridge, an employee of Chauncey Jerome.
1836	Joseph Shaylor Ives invented a process for making brass coil springs.
1837	Financial crisis spread across America. Dollar fell.
1837	Chauncey Jerome introduced a one-day brass movement in an ogee case that sold for $1.50.
c 1840	Tall case clocks ceased to be made.
1840	Spring fusees introduced by Charles Kirk.
1841	Beehive clock introduced. Designed by Elias Ingraham, made by E. C. Brewster.
1841	Aaron Dodd Crane granted patent for torsion pendulum clock.
c 1841	Joseph Ives introduced the hour glass clock.

1842	America's first export of clocks. Chauncey Jerome shipped cheap ogee clocks to England.
1843	Charles Kirk invented cast iron back plate with integral spring wells.
1844	Elias Ingraham designed steeple clock case.
c 1845	Connecticut clockmakers achieved world supremacy in clock production.
1845	Jonathan Clark Brown of Forestville Manufacturing Co. introduced the acorn clock.
1847	Steel coil springs became available.
c 1848	William Barnbridge Barnes introduced a 30-hour brass movement with a spring balance wheel. Later known as marine or lever movement.
1850	Steel coil springs were attached directly to the great wheel arbor without fusees.
1859	Joseph Ives introduced the tin plate movement.
1861-1865	American Civil War.
1863	Theodore R. Timby patented his solar timepiece.
1875	Seth Thomas Sons & Co. introduced marine movements in small, round alarm clocks.

APPENDIX 3

Bibliography of Useful Books and Journals

BOOKS

American Clocks and Clock Makers* *by Carl W. Drepperd* (pub. 1958 by C.T. Branford Co., 19 Calvin Road, Box 16, Watertown, MA 02172)

Simon Willard and His Clocks *by John Ware Willard* (pub. 1968 by Dover Publications, Inc., 180 Varick St., New York, NY 10014)

The Contributions of Joseph Ives to Connecticut Clock Technology 1810-1862 *by Kenneth D. Roberts* (pub. 1970 by American Clock & Watch Museum Inc., 100 Maple St., Bristol, CT 06109)

The American Clock* *by William H. Distin and Robert Bishop* (pub. 1976 by E.P. Dutton & Co., Inc., 201 Park Avenue South, New York, NY 10003)

Eli Terry and the Connecticut Shelf Clock *by Kenneth D. Roberts* (pub. 1973 by Ken Roberts Publishing Co, Bristol, CT 06010)

A Treasury of American Clocks* *by Brooks Palmer* (pub. 1967 by Macmillan Publishing Co., Inc., 866 Third Avenue, New York, NY 10022)

The Book of American Clocks* *by Brooks Palmer* (pub. 1974 by Macmillan Publishing Co., Inc., 866 Third Avenue, New York, NY 10022)

Two Hundred Years of American Clocks and Watches* *by Chris H. Bailey* (pub. 1975 by Prentice-Hall Inc., Englewood Cliffs, NJ 07632)

**These books include a list of makers*

JOURNALS

Bulletin of the National Association of Watch and Clock Collectors, Inc., (Available to members only: application to N.A.W.C.C., P.O. Box 33, Columbia, PA 17512)

Antiquarian Horology (Available to members only: application to The Antiquarian Horological Society, New House, High Street, Ticehurst, Wadhurst, Sussex TN5 7AL, England)

American Horologist & Jeweler (2403 Champa St., Denver, CO 80205)

INDEX